GREAT MYSTERIES

The Assassination of Abraham Lincoln

OPPOSING VIEWPOINTS®

Look for these and other exciting *Great Mysteries: Opposing Viewpoints* books:

GREAT MYSTERIES

The Assassination of Abraham Lincoln

OPPOSING VIEWPOINTS®

by Michael O'Neal

Greenhaven Press, Inc.   P.O. Box 289009, San Diego, California 92198-0009

Library of Congress Cataloging-in-Publication Data

O'Neal, Michael, 1949-
   The assassination of Abraham Lincoln : opposing viewpoints / by Michael O'Neal.
     p. cm. — (Great mysteries)
   Includes bibliographical references and index.
   Summary: Explores the mysteries that still surround the death of President Lincoln.
   ISBN 0-89908-092-8 (Lib.)
   1. Lincoln, Abraham, 1809-1865 — Assassination — Juvenile literature. [1. Lincoln, Abraham, 1809-1865 — Assassination.] I. Title. II. Series: Great mysteries.
F547.5.O5 1991
364.1'524'092—dc20   91-13682

To Bill O.,
Southern gentleman and Dad

Contents

Introduction

This book is written for the curious—those who want to explore the mysteries that are everywhere. To be human is to be constantly surrounded by wonderment. How do birds fly? Are ghosts real? Can animals and people communicate? Was King Arthur a real person or a myth? Why did Amelia Earhart disappear? Did history really happen the way we think it did? Where did the world come from? Where is it going?

Great Mysteries: Opposing Viewpoints books are intended to offer the reader an opportunity to explore some of the many mysteries that both trouble and intrigue us. For the span of each book, we want the reader to feel that he or she is a scientist investigating the extinction of the dinosaurs, an archaeologist searching for clues to the origin of the great Egyptian pyramids, a psychic detective testing the existence of ESP.

One thing all mysteries have in common is that there is no ready answer. Often there are *many* answers but none on which even the majority of authorities agrees. *Great Mysteries: Opposing Viewpoints* books introduce the intriguing views of the experts, allowing the reader to participate in their explorations, their theories, and their disagreements as they try to explain the mysteries of our world.

But most readers won't want to stop here. These *Great Mysteries: Opposing Viewpoints* aim to stimulate the reader's curiosity. Although truth is often impossible to discover, the search is fascinating. It is up to the reader to examine the evidence, to decide whether the answer is there—or to explore further.

"Penetrating so many secrets, we cease to believe in the unknowable. But there it sits nevertheless, calmly licking its chops."

H.L. Mencken, American essayist

Prologue

In 1956, Mr. Samuel J. Seymour of Arlington, Virginia, died at the age of ninety-six.

Mr. Seymour was not in any way a famous person. His death was not widely noted. It is likely that the only people who have any distinct remembrances of him are the members of his family, his friends, and perhaps some co-workers.

Yet in its own way, Mr. Seymour's quiet death marked the passing of an era—and the end of a dramatic story known to every American citizen. For as far as can be determined, Mr. Seymour was the last surviving person to have attended Ford's Theatre in Washington, D.C., on the evening of April 14, 1865. There he witnessed one of the most tragic events in American history, one that has left behind a tangled legacy of unanswered, perhaps unanswerable, questions.

The young Seymour was at Ford's with his godmother to see the celebrated actress, Laura Keene, in a popular comedy by Tom Taylor called *Our American Cousin*. But this trip to the theater promised to be no ordinary one. Earlier in the day, playbills had circulated around the capital announcing that President Abraham Lincoln and his wife Mary Lincoln would be attending the play, and the

(opposite page) Abraham Lincoln became the sixteenth president of the United States in 1861. He was assassinated four years later by John Wilkes Booth. Did Booth act alone or was he part of a conspiracy?

afternoon newspapers reported that with them would be the Civil War hero, Gen. Ulysses S. Grant. Just five years old at the time, Seymour probably had no particular interest in the play. But to catch a glimpse of President Lincoln and General Grant—now that would be something to remember!

A Pop Is Heard

The play began at 7:45. The president's party arrived about forty-five minutes later. At about a quarter after ten, the actor Harry Hawk, playing the part of a penniless country bumpkin, was on stage alone. The audience broke into laughter at his response to the haughty claim of Mrs. Mountchessington that he is not used to the manners of polite society: "Don't know the manners of good society, eh? Well, I guess I know enough to turn you inside out, old gal—you sockdologizing old mantrap." As the laughter subsided, young Seymour heard a pop,

This lithograph, published in *Harper's Weekly*, shows the nation mourning the slain president.

described later by members of the audience as sounding like the explosion of a blown-up paper bag. Suddenly, something entirely unexpected occurred: A man carrying a knife leapt from the president's box at the right of the stage. He landed off balance with his back to the audience, but he quickly regained his feet, flourished his knife, and shouted "Sic semper tyrannis!" (which in Latin means "thus always to tyrants"). He then ran off the stage to the left.

The audience was stunned, though some later said they first thought it was part of the play. But soon the screams of Mrs. Lincoln made it frighteningly clear to all what had happened—the president of the United States had just been shot!

Soon, word spread throughout Washington that the president was mortally wounded by an assassin's bullet—and the assassin was none other than the famous young actor, John Wilkes Booth. Days later, Booth would be killed trying to elude capture. His accomplices were soon caught, tried, and hanged. But almost immediately, suspicions arose that Booth's little group had not acted alone, that they had had the backing and help of important people who had their own reasons for wanting Lincoln dead.

While no one doubts that Booth pulled the trigger, the question persists to this day: Who really was responsible for the death of President Abraham Lincoln?

One

The Tragedy at Ford's Theatre

Good Friday, April 14, 1865, brought to a close a week of jubilation in Washington, D.C. For four years, the nation had been torn apart by a bloody civil war, the "War between the States," that had sometimes torn even families apart. But finally, on April 9, the leader of the main Confederate Army, Gen. Robert E. Lee, had surrendered to General Grant at Appomattox Court House in Virginia. Cannons and fireworks in the capital announced the end of the nation's agony. The mood in Washington was one of elation and hope for the future. That mood was destined to be short-lived.

The president rose that morning to a warm and sunny day. After breakfast, he turned to the day's business. Much of his morning was taken up meeting with various callers. One was Senator John P. Hale, whom Lincoln had recently appointed ambassador to Spain. During their conversation, Hale told the president that he was glad to have the post. It would enable him to remove his young daughter Bessie from the influence of a notorious actor. The actor's name was John Wilkes Booth.

Some time after 10:00, the president remembered that he had promised Mrs. Lincoln they would go to the theater that evening. He sent a mes-

senger over to Ford's Theatre to reserve the presidential box. The day before he had asked General Grant to accompany them. Grant had seemed a bit evasive and unsure, but he accepted the invitation, so the president asked that a seat in the box also be reserved for Grant.

The main order of business for the day came at 11:00. A cabinet meeting had been called to discuss the end of the war and to enable cabinet officials to confer with General Grant, the hero of the hour. Absent was Secretary of State William Seward, who was at home in Lafayette Square, just minutes from the White House, recovering from injuries he had suffered in a carriage accident. Despite his incapacity, Seward was fated to play a role in events later that day.

The cabinet immediately turned its attention to the war. Although Lee had surrendered, Confederate troops under the command of Gen. Joseph Johnston were still resisting—at least as far as anyone could know in days when lines of communication were slow and uncertain. Grant pointed out that he

The nation suffered many losses as a result of the bloody Civil War. Here, a soldier lies dead in an open trench, one of thousands of victims of the war's skirmishes and battles.

had not heard from Gen. William Sherman, the Union general in pursuit of Johnston and his forces. The president stated his hope that news of Johnston's surrender would soon arrive, perhaps that very day.

Forgiveness and Reconciliation

The future of the nation was on the minds of everyone present. If the war really was ending, the victorious North needed to consider its postwar policy toward the South. Some cabinet officials expressed the hope that the leaders of the Confederacy, including its president, Jefferson Davis, would flee the country. Their flight would relieve the North of the painful duty of prosecuting them. Lincoln took the opportunity to repeat his hope that the North would deal with the South in a spirit of forgiveness and reconciliation: "I hope there will be no persecution, no bloody work after the war is over. No one need expect me to take any part in hanging or killing these men, even the worst of them." At the request of the president, Secretary of War Edwin M. Stanton then presented a report on ways to rebuild the South and bring it back into the Union. Thus began what would be a long day for the president's eccentric war secretary.

When the meeting ended some time between 1:30 and 2:00, Grant lingered to express to the president his regrets that he would be unable to attend the theater that evening. Neither of the two men knew that the afternoon newspapers were already reporting that Grant would be at Ford's with Lincoln. The result would be a packed house on a day—Good Friday—that was normally a slow one for theaters. Although it is unclear why Grant declined the president's invitation, it was common knowledge that both Grant and his wife disliked Mrs. Lincoln.

The president returned to his office after lunch. Following meetings with Vice President Andrew

"This assassination is not the act of one man."

Edward Bates, Lincoln's attorney general

"Booth himself was . . . the projector and animating soul of the monstrous plot."

Journalist Horace Greeley

Johnson and Assistant Secretary of War Charles Dana, he made good on a promise to Mrs. Lincoln to take a carriage ride and enjoy part of the warm spring afternoon. He found the festive mood of the capital city catching. At one point during the ride, he turned to his wife and said, "I never felt so happy in my life. . . . I consider that this day the War has come to an end. We must both be cheerful in the future."

After the carriage ride, though, the president's spirits seemed less buoyant. He walked to the War Department to see if there was news on the wire from General Sherman. On the way back to the White House, he remarked to his bodyguard, "Do you know, I believe there are men who want to take my life. And I have no doubt they will do it." Perhaps at that moment, Lincoln was thinking of the envelope he kept on his desk containing eighty of the death threats he had received. What would he have thought had he known of the hundreds of others his staff had intercepted? He went on to comment that he had no real desire to attend the theater. The only reason he was still going was that the newspapers had already announced he would be there. He did not want to disappoint members of the audience who wanted to see the president as much as the play.

To the Theater

After dinner, the president had further meetings with various political figures. He apparently had a hard time getting away from his last visitor, for it was not until about 8:10 that the presidential carriage left the White House. The Lincolns' first stop was the home of Senator Ira Harris, whose daughter Clara would be attending the play with them, accompanied by her fiancé, Maj. Henry R. Rathbone. At about 8:30, the party arrived at Ford's, where the play was already underway. They ascended the stairs leading to the balcony and proceeded down a short corridor to the presidential box overlooking the stage.

With the arrival of the Lincolns, the play stopped and the orchestra struck up "Hail to the Chief." In response to the cheers and applause of the audience, the president came to the front of the box, smiled, and bowed. Clara Harris seated herself at the front of the box to the right; Major Rathbone took a seat on a small sofa just behind her to her left. Mrs. Lincoln was to their left, while the president sat on the far left, out of sight of most of the audience, in an upholstered rocking chair. The play resumed, and the president remained absorbed in it for the next hour and a half. He seemed to enjoy this time of relaxation before resuming the task of healing the nation.

Enter the Assassin

Sometime between 9:30 and 10:00, a horse picked its way down Baptist Alley, behind Ford's Theatre. Its rider was John Wilkes Booth. While one of the stagehands held his horse, Booth entered the rear of the theater, crossed beneath the stage to an exit near the front, and went into a tavern adjoining the theater on the south side. As he sat at the bar, he was recognized by a drunken patron, who raised a glass and said, "You'll never be the actor your father was." Rather than taking offense, Booth smiled and replied, "When I leave the stage, I will be the most famous man in America."

Booth reentered the theater and was seen several times in the lobby. Shortly after 10:00, he ascended the stairs to the balcony and proceeded to the corridor leading to the president's box. He opened the door that separated the corridor from the balcony area and entered the corridor. After closing the door, he jammed it shut with a piece of lumber he had hidden earlier in the day.

As an actor, Booth had performed in *Our American Cousin* many times, so he knew when the stage

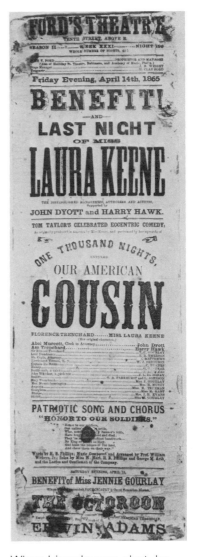

When Lincoln was shot, he was seated at Ford's Theatre in Washington, D.C., attending a performance of *Our American Cousin*. Shown here is Lincoln's bloodstained program.

When Lincoln entered Ford's Theatre on the night of his death, the play halted and the band struck up "Hail to the Chief." Lincoln walked to the front of the presidential box, smiled, and bowed to the audience.

would be empty save for Harry Hawk. He waited for his cue. When he heard the words "you sockdologizing old mantrap," he knew the moment had come. He silently opened the unguarded door to the president's box, approached the president, and at close range fired the fatal shot. The president slumped forward in his chair and never regained consciousness.

Major Rathbone heard the shot and saw the cloud of smoke. He leapt at the assassin. Booth dropped the murder weapon, a .44-caliber derringer, and slashed at the major with his knife, wounding him in the arm. He then vaulted over the railing of the box. His spur, though, caught on one of the flags draped over the railing, so he landed awkwardly, breaking a bone in his left leg. In spite of the pain, he strode across the stage to the left, exited the theater, mounted his horse, and rode away into the Washington night before he could be stopped.

Inside, pandemonium broke loose. Several doctors in the audience rushed to the president's aid. They could see, though, that the wound was mortal. They carried the president to the street and from there to the nearby house of William Petersen. Throughout the night, doctors, members of the cabinet, and others kept watch at the president's bedside, but it was clear to all that there was no hope. At 7:22 on the morning of April 15, 1865, the president died. At his bedside was Secretary Stanton, who is said at that moment to have uttered the words, "Now he belongs to the ages."

Escape from Washington

Mounted on his horse, Booth raced through the misty streets of Washington to the Navy Yard Bridge. There he was met by an accomplice, David Herold, and the two made their escape from the capital city. The bridge was supposed to be closed after dark, but the guard saw nothing wrong with letting the famous Mr. Booth pass. Heading toward the safety of the South, the fugitives stopped briefly at a tavern in Surrattsville, Maryland, to pick up a package containing a gun. A few hours later they reached the home of Dr. Samuel Mudd, who tended to Booth's broken leg.

The next day, Booth and Herold continued their flight through the Maryland and Virginia countryside until they reached the home of Richard H. Garrett near Port Royal, Virginia, on the afternoon of April 24. At about 2:00 A.M. on April 26, a Union cavalry detachment tracked Booth and Herold to Garrett's barn. Herold gave up, but Booth resisted, so the cavalry set fire to the barn. Booth appeared briefly in an open doorway and was shot. He died a few hours later.

This outline of the main events surrounding the Lincoln assassination tells only part of the story, for Booth had planned a crime whose scope was to extend beyond the murder of the president, and he enlisted the help of a ragtag band of accomplices. One, David Herold, a young drugstore clerk, has already been mentioned. Another more sinister figure was Louis Paine, a hulking, silent man who originally was to have accompanied Booth to Ford's to kill Grant. But when Booth learned during the afternoon of April 14 that Grant would not be at the theater, he ordered Paine to kill Secretary Seward at his home instead. Paine tried to carry out his role. At about 10:00, while Booth was lingering in the

The fatally wounded president was carried to the nearby house of William Petersen. There, doctors, cabinet members, and others kept watch at his bedside throughout the night. The president died at 7:22 the next morning.

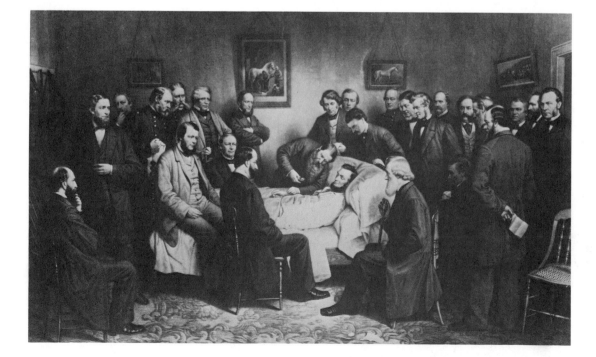

lobby at Ford's, Paine arrived at Seward's house in Lafayette Square, claiming he was delivering medicine. He attacked Seward's son, fracturing his skull, then entered Seward's bedroom and stabbed the secretary twice. But Seward was wearing around his head and neck a cumbersome steel brace, which blocked Paine's thrusts and probably saved Seward's life.

A third accomplice was George Atzerodt, a scruffy-looking German immigrant who would agree to do anything for a price. Atzerodt was boarding at the Kirkwood House, where one of his fellow boarders was Vice President Johnson. Atzerodt's task was to kill the vice president at the same time Booth was killing the president. But at the appointed moment he lost his nerve and got drunk. He spent much of the night wandering around the city, finally checking into a rundown boarding house at the same time Johnson was visiting the dying president.

The role of another conspirator has never been entirely clear. Mary Surratt was a widow who ran a Washington boarding house. Her son, John Surratt, was a Confederate spy and "blockade runner"—that is, he smuggled cargo and supplies into the South through Northern naval blockades. He liked the atmosphere of intrigue and danger surrounding Booth. John Surratt, Paine, Herold, Atzerodt, and Booth all met frequently to discuss their plans at Mary Surratt's boarding house, and she was the one who took the package containing the gun to her family's hometown of Surrattsville, where Booth retrieved it on the night of his flight.

By the time Booth was killed on April 26, the authorities had rounded up these and other conspirators.

The Aftermath of Violence

It would be hard to exaggerate the profound effect that Lincoln's assassination had on the nation. Even during his life, but perhaps more so after his death, the president came to be viewed as a larger-than-life hero. This does not mean that everyone revered the president. The Civil War had created intense bitterness and distrust between many parts of American society: North versus South, slave owners versus abolitionists (those who wanted to "abolish" slavery), industry versus agriculture, those who believed in the supremacy of the national government versus those who favored the rights of the individual states. In this tense climate, many people hated Lincoln; some had even openly declared that his death would be good for the nation.

Nonetheless, "Father Abraham," as he was often called, seemed to be the only person capable of reuniting the country. He symbolized the hope that the North and South would again be one. The words in which he expressed that hope still stir us: "With malice toward none; with charity for all; with firmness in the right, as God gives us to see the right, let us strive on to finish the work we are in; . . . to do all which may achieve and cherish a just and lasting peace among ourselves, and with all nations."

No Strong Leader

Throughout the North, the immediate response to the president's death was one almost of panic. Because the assassination was the work of a Southerner, it seemed clear to many that it was the prelude to one last desperate attempt by the Confederacy to regroup its forces and attack the North—now lacking a strong leader. When the panic subsided, it was replaced by a mood that was nearly as dangerous—one of outrage and a thirst for vengeance. Hopes for an early reconciliation between North and South were dashed.

This was the atmosphere in which Booth was hunted down and shot and his accomplices rounded up. As the president lay dying during the early morning hours of April 15, Secretary Stanton was beginning to take testimony from witnesses, order protection for other public officials, and draw the

Although John Wilkes Booth fired the bullet that killed Lincoln, Booth was not alone in carrying out the president's assassination. He enlisted a ragtag group of accomplices to assist him.

net around the conspirators. The government offered huge rewards for their capture, and the press published accounts of the murder that stressed the Southern connections of the plotters. After they were caught, the government did not waste any time. On May 9, 1865, the conspirators—all civilians—were charged before a special military court. As a group, they were charged with conspiring to assassinate Lincoln, Grant, Seward, and Johnson. Also named in the charges were Jefferson Davis and other Confederate leaders.

Guilty as Charged

On June 30, after a sensational six-week trial, the court found all of the defendants guilty as charged. Dr. Mudd and other minor conspirators were sentenced to prison, but they were pardoned by President Johnson in 1869. John Surratt had fled to Europe, but was finally captured in Egypt, brought home, and tried in 1867 in a civilian court.

The War Department offered a $100,000 reward for the apprehension of Booth and two of his accomplices, John H. Surratt and David C. Herold.

When the jury was unable to reach a verdict, his case was dismissed.

On July 6, 1865, Paine, Herold, Atzerodt, and Mary Surratt were informed of their sentences. Less than twenty-four hours later, on July 7, they were hanged in the yard of the Washington Arsenal. The public's thirst for quick and sure retribution was quenched.

Historian Vaughan Shelton summarizes the version of events that people have generally accepted over the past century:

> A humanitarian president who had successfully steered his country through a bloody civil war was murdered by an insane actor to avenge the defeat of the Southern Confederacy. Twelve days later, after a countrywide search, the actor was traced to a farm . . . and was shot to death by a Union cavalryman when he refused to surrender. The actor's gang of accomplices was rounded up and—after a trial of several weeks, in which they had every opportunity to defend themselves—were sentenced.

This is the version of events that has passed into the history books.

Sealed Records

But almost immediately, people began to raise questions about the assassination and its aftermath. They challenged the "official" version of events that Secretary of War Stanton and other government authorities promoted. Over the following decades, many people involved with the tragedy published their accounts of it. The contradictions among many of these accounts contributed to the mystery and uncertainty surrounding Lincoln's death. And the fact that all of the government's records of the conspiracy trial were sealed in War Department archives until the 1930s has fueled speculation that the "real" story was covered up. Virtually every "fact" connected with Lincoln's death and the capture and trial of the conspirators has been examined. Investigators have asked many questions and offered many theories. All of these questions combined have left historians with one great mystery: Who was really responsible for the death of the president?

Many historians place the origin of the assassination plot squarely on Booth's shoulders. Others, however, argue that Booth was only a tool, a puppet acting under the directions of others. The evidence is not conclusive, but historians who maintain that the conspiracy extended beyond Booth and his gang begin with a number of intriguing questions:

Why was the president of the United States sitting *unprotected* in a public theater, in light of the hundreds of vicious death threats he had received? Was the president deliberately betrayed?

Why were the civilian conspirators tried by a military tribunal for no clear reason? Was the conspiracy trial rigged? Was Mary Surratt, in particular, the victim of what protestors called "judicial murder"?

How far did the conspiracy extend? Did it include high-ranking officials in the Confederacy? Could it have included high-ranking *Union* figures, including members of the president's own party?

Does any solid evidence support the most horrifying possibility of all: Could Vice President Andrew Johnson have had a hand in Lincoln's death? Was the plot to kill Lincoln masterminded by high-ranking members of Lincoln's own administration?

Two

What Motivated John Wilkes Booth to Kill the President?

The word "assassin" conjures up a picture of a disturbed figure, lurking in the shadows, waiting to strike his or her target, or of a crazed fanatic, whose murderous actions grow from twisted, irrational motives that "normal" people find impossible to understand.

Neither of these descriptions fits John Wilkes Booth. He was no lone gunman who crept, unknown and unseen, out of the back alleys of Washington to enter his name in U.S. history books. He was a well-known, highly recognizable public figure. His very name on a playbill could fill theaters throughout the South and many in the North. He enjoyed the acclaim of thousands of fans. His charm with both men and women was legendary. If he had lived in the twentieth century, he would no doubt have been described with words like "superstar" and "heartthrob," and his face would surely have adorned the covers of fan magazines.

Born in 1838, John Wilkes was the ninth of ten children born out of wedlock to Junius Brutus Booth and Mary Ann Holmes. First in Virginia, then in northern Maryland, he grew up as the spoiled, pampered son of one of the most famous Shakespearean actors in the history of American

(opposite page) Some historians contend that as the years passed, Lincoln became a storybook hero. His assassin, in turn, has been described as a monstrous devil and madman. In this illustration, the devil tempts Booth to kill Lincoln, who is seated in the background.

President Lincoln's carriage arrived in front of Ford's Theatre (center), on Washington's Tenth Street, about forty-five minutes after the beginning of *Our American Cousin*. Less than two hours later, the president was shot in the back of the head and fatally wounded.

theater. By the 1860s, Booth had fame, money, and the opportunity to make a permanent name for himself in a glamorous profession. Why did he sacrifice these advantages—and his life—to become a political assassin? Historians and biographers have remained intrigued with this question, for efforts to know the "real" Booth have proven futile.

In his turn-of-the-century biography, *Myths After Lincoln*, Lloyd Lewis shows that as time went on and Lincoln became in the popular mind a kind of storybook hero, Booth had to be described as a monstrous devil and madman. But many of Booth's biographers, including Clare Laughlin and even Carl Sandburg, paint a more sympathetic portrait. Their Booth is a likable, good-humored, spirited man who may have truly feared that Lincoln was a tyrant, and who merely acted on anti-Lincoln beliefs that had been openly stated in both the South and the North. Between these extremes can be found a variety of explanations for the most infamous crime of the century.

Booth the Madman

One tradition holds that when Booth pulled the trigger in Ford's Theatre, he was a lunatic, a madman who had finally stumbled across a chance to carry out a spectacular murder.

Stanley Kimmel is one biographer who takes

Booth was a famous actor. His name alone on a playbill could fill theaters.

Some historians believe Booth was a disturbed man who harbored a deep hatred for his father. This hatred may have extended to his brother Edwin, who was also an actor. Edwin, who went on to stardom, is seen here portraying Hamlet.

this position. In *The Mad Booths of Maryland,* Kimmel points to the mental imbalance of Junius Booth and the effects that it had on young John Wilkes. Even on the stage, Junius showed signs of the weakness he would pass on to his son. Several of his colleagues, for example, fled from the stage during performances of *Richard III,* convinced he was actually trying to kill them during the play's famous dueling scene. Once, actors had to save the heroine Desdemona from Junius's crazed Othello when they thought he was actually trying to smother her with a pillow in the play's climactic scene. Almost as legendary as his stage performances was his hard drinking. Frequently, Junius appeared on stage drunk. Often he began a performance sober enough, but drank between scenes to the point that he could hardly finish the show. This father often was away from home on theatrical tours and would return at uncertain intervals to dominate his family.

A Disturbed Man

John Wilkes seemed to have inherited some of his father's mental imbalance. Early in life, he showed signs of a violent temper. He was often sullen and depressed. He would shoot dogs and cats for no reason. He, too, became a hard drinker, able to put away brandy by the bottle.

But some of Booth's biographers have taken these details of his early life one step further. In their view, Booth's motives are so obscure that only modern psychology can explain them. The first of these "psychological" biographers was Philip Van Doren Stern, writing in the 1930s. He was followed by George W. Wilson, Edward J. Kempf, and Philip Weissman. All of these writers "examined" Booth as if he were a patient, and all arrived at similar conclusions.

Booth, they say, was a disturbed man who for years had borne a deep-seated hatred for his father.

This hatred may have extended to his brother Edwin. To the young John Wilkes, Junius Booth was an unreliable, drunken tyrant, never to be counted on for anything except to thwart John's own desire to be an actor. Edwin, who went on to stardom, stole John's "rightful" place not only in their father's affections, but on stage as well.

When Junius died in 1852, John Wilkes no longer had a target for his hatred. It seethed in him until 1865, these writers say, when it erupted against a substitute father, "Father Abraham" Lincoln. Like many Southerners, Booth saw Lincoln as a cruel and despicable tyrant, a kind of self-appointed "king," drunk with power, who had declared war on Booth's homeland. And he was the kind of figure that Booth night after night symbolically put to death on stage in some of his tragic roles. Thus, when Booth shot Lincoln, he was acting out a mad desire to kill his own father.

For historian William Hanchett, these theories are based on false assumptions. Citing evidence from diaries and autobiographies written by members of the Booth family, Hanchett challenges the view that Booth hated or resented his father. He believes that the evidence shows the opposite—that Booth idolized his father. And, if Junius resisted John's desire for an acting career, he resisted Edwin's, too, wanting all his children to lead a normal life. To Hanchett, the psychological explanations for Booth's crime are "nonsense."

A Lust for Fame

Other historians and biographers have taken a different path in trying to understand Booth's complex personality. With Osborn Oldroyd, they believe that the driving force behind Booth's actions was not insanity, but a desire "solely to immortalize himself." While both views suggest mental imbalance, Booth's craving for fame and immortality, in Oldroyd's view, stemmed less from specific events

"A Confederate Doing Duty upon His Own Responsibility."
John Wilkes Booth, signature to a letter

"Being a very vain, superficial person . . . Booth must have had some motivation other than Southern patriotism."
Historian Vaughan Shelton

"It was the act of a madman, driven insane by the sudden collapse of his patriotic ambition, the maddening fear of the total failure of cherished plans to save his country—and by the sudden exaggeration of hereditary imbalance."

Francis Wilson, Booth biographer

"Booth was not a madman; he believed he had good reasons to take Lincoln's life. He was not alone."

Historian William Hanchett

of his childhood and more from his own personality. These biographers point to an eerily prophetic remark Booth made to a group of school chums during a discussion of the Colossus of Rhodes, one of the Seven Wonders of the World: "Suppose that statue was now standing and I should, by some means, overthrow it. My name would descend to posterity and never be forgotten, for it would be in all the histories of the times, and be read thousands of years after we are dead." In a way, Booth would get his ominous wish.

The desire to become a legend seemed even to influence Booth's acting style. He began his stage career in 1856, at age eighteen, with no real training. Never gifted with eloquence or a smooth stage voice, Booth relied instead not only on his dashing good looks, but on energy, passion, and spectacular effects—though some critics found his style clumsy and exaggerated. It was characteristic of Booth that for a performance of *Macbeth* at Ford's Theatre he made leaping entrances onto the stage from a twelve-foot-high ledge of rocks he had erected. Ironically, the president's box, from which Booth leapt to the stage on the night of the assassination, was twelve feet above the stage.

Vague Impulses

For Booth, the surest way to sign his name in the history books was through the theater. But the dividing line between the fantasies of the stage and the realities of life was never very clear to him. Thus, in his offstage life he was driven by the same vague impulses that governed his acting. During the late 1850s, for example, he belonged to a political organization called the Know-Nothing Party. The Know-Nothings were an organization of fanatics who stood for a twisted, flag-waving patriotism. When asked about their party, members would respond, "I know nothing." They took great enjoyment in breaking up political meetings, badgering

Catholic priests, setting fires, and inciting riots. Most important, they appealed to a boyish love of secret societies.

Booth reveled in this sort of activity—a world of passwords, coded messages, and secret handshakes. It was the stuff of melodrama, a nighttime world of cloaks and daggers. This was the Booth described by historian Vaughan Shelton: "In conversation, in letter-writing, in any of the ordinary communications of living, he was never offstage and just himself. . . . In this manner the necessary boundary between art and reality was gradually erased, and he was unable to distinguish between the two." Shelton describes Booth's scheme for kidnapping the president in similar terms, calling it "the script for a blood and thunder melodrama."

Booth the Confederate Spy

Some historians remain intrigued with a third possible motive: that Booth was on the payroll of the Confederacy as a spy acting under orders.

If Booth was a spy, he certainly did not always play the part. A spy, for example, would have kept to himself instead of openly declaring his anti-North, anti-Lincoln sentiments. No spy would have given a speech in New York in the first days of the Civil War praising the heroism of the South. Nor would he have declared at a Chicago theater, "What a glorious opportunity there is for a man to immortalize himself by killing Lincoln."

Historian Theodore Roscoe argues that Booth's position as a public figure actually gave him the cover he needed. As an actor, he traveled freely among cities in the North, with the help of a pass signed by General Grant. He thus had plenty of opportunity to meet with members of the network of spies the South had placed in cities throughout the North. In New York, Baltimore, Philadelphia, Washington, and a score of other cities, he spent part of each evening wrapped in the robes of the

Gen. Ulysses S. Grant signed a pass that enabled Booth to travel freely among cities in the North.

Shakespearean characters he portrayed. The curtain would fall, to rise later—in a tavern, a dark alley, or a seedy hotel room—on Booth, wrapped in the robes of a Southern spy.

It is unclear how deeply involved Booth might have been with the highly organized Confederate secret service, the "Gray Underground," so called because of the gray uniform worn by the Confederate army. But Roscoe points to indirect evidence that Booth was an active spy. In 1864, for example, he played several engagements in Niagara Falls, New York, a hotbed of Southern espionage. The city is just over the border from Canada, not far from Montreal. Montreal was the headquarters for the "Canadian Cabinet," a group of Confederate leaders who directed spy and sabotage operations

President Lincoln discusses strategy in the field during the Civil War. Some historians contend that Booth saw himself as a Southern patriot who hoped to eliminate President Lincoln so that the Confederacy might regroup and attack the leaderless Union.

against Northern cities from across the border.

By itself, all this would mean little. But Booth left a trail of sabotage in cities where he played. One of the most notorious incidents took place in New York City on November 25, 1864. That night, fires broke out in several large Manhattan hotels. Investigation proved that this arson raid was the work of Southern agents. One agent was captured and confessed that the plot was directed by the Canadian Cabinet. Booth's movements place him in Canada in the days preceding the arson raid, meeting with these Southern leaders. No evidence links Booth directly to the fires. But to Roscoe, the sequence of events suggests strongly that Booth used his access to cities in the North as a way to pass messages and information. Unfortunately, the extent of Booth's involvement in the Gray Underground will probably never be known. When Richmond, Virginia, fell on April 9, 1865, most of the records detailing the actions of the Confederate secret service were destroyed.

The War Department, under Secretary of War Edwin M. Stanton, offered $50,000 for the capture of Booth.

Booth the Southern Patriot

By 1864, the tide of war had turned against the South. One of the key factors was the size of the Confederate army. The North had a larger population, and thus more troops. Secretary of War Stanton and General Grant pressed this advantage by ending the policy of trading prisoners of war with the South. At that time, the North held 50,000 Southern prisoners, and thousands more were added during the campaigns of 1864. The South desperately needed these troops to carry on the fight.

Whether Booth was officially on the rolls as a Southern agent, historians agree that he clearly saw himself as a patriot, acting on the South's behalf. Accordingly, he began to form a solution to the troop problem. But his plan at first was not to kill the president. It was to kidnap him and carry him to Richmond. There, Lincoln would be held as a

In the plot to kidnap the president, George Atzerodt was supposed to ferry the kidnapping party across the Potomac to the safety of Virginia. The plot was never carried out.

hostage, to be released in exchange for Confederate prisoners of war.

Having conceived this bold plan, he set to work.

Hatching the Plot

Booth's first step was to recruit his gang of accomplices. Each had qualifications that suited him for the job. Atzerodt was a carriage painter from the little town of Port Tobacco, Maryland. But he moonlighted as an underground boatman, smuggling blockade runners across the Potomac River. Herold, the drugstore clerk, not only idolized Booth but was an avid hunter who knew every inch of the swampy country of lower Maryland and could thus serve as a guide during Booth's escape. Paine provided the muscle. By nature a violent man, he could be counted on if matters got rough. And there were other minor figures. Michael O'Laughlin and Samuel B. Arnold, ex-Confederate soldiers, were both pals from Booth's school days. With this pair, Booth hatched the abduction plot over brandy in a Baltimore hotel. Later, when he set up his Washington base of operations in Mary Surratt's boarding house, Booth became acquainted with John Surratt, an eager supporter of the kidnap scheme. In the meantime, he recruited Ned Spangler, the stagehand who later would wait with Booth's horse in Baptist Alley behind Ford's Theatre while Booth assassinated the president.

One Eye on Lincoln

His pawns gathered, Booth kept one eye on Lincoln, waiting for the right time to make his move. But as usual he kept the other eye on the spectacular effect—for he had decided to carry out the kidnapping in a theater!

Booth planned two separate kidnap attempts. Each was a disaster. The first was in January 1865 when Booth heard of the president's plan to attend a performance of *Jack Cade* at Ford's. Spangler was

The Surratt boardinghouse in Washington, D.C., served as Booth's base of operations.

to turn off the gas valve, leaving the theater in darkness. Led by Booth, who of course knew his way around the building, Surratt and Paine were to burst in, seize the president, tie him up, and spirit him off—all before anyone had the presence of mind to stop them. Herold would then guide the "capture" party through the backwaters of southern Maryland, while Atzerodt would be waiting in Port Tobacco with a boat to ferry the party across the Potomac, the last obstacle between Washington and Richmond.

The plot never got under way. On the night of the play, a terrible storm hit the capital and at the last minute Lincoln decided to stay home. The conspirators scattered, fearing that the president had changed his plans because the plot had been discovered. Booth, though, waited for another chance.

It came in March. Rallying his accomplices for another try, he unfolded his plan: to ambush the president while he was on his way to Campbell Hospital, a home for wounded soldiers near the capital, where Lincoln frequently attended benefit stage performances.

Once again, the drama turned into a farce. Booth

Samuel Arnold, a commissary clerk and ex-Confederate soldier, was Booth's friend from school days. Arnold helped formulate the plan to kidnap the president.

Southern gentlemen survey war-torn Richmond, the capital of the Confederacy. After Richmond fell, the Confederate army surrendered, dashing Booth's patriotic ambitions.

and the other conspirators lurked in a grove of trees on the road to the home. As a carriage rounded a bend, Booth and Surratt rode down the road on horseback toward the home, acting like chance travelers. As the presidential carriage drove between them, Booth peered in—to discover that the president was not inside! Had Booth read the newspaper that day, he would have known that the president had canceled his plan to attend the matinee at Campbell's to attend instead a ceremonial flag presentation—which took place on the street outside the Washington hotel where Booth was staying!

On April 9, 1865, at Virginia's Appomattox Courthouse, Gen. Ulysses S. Grant (center, at table) and other Union leaders watch Confederate Gen. Robert E. Lee sign the surrender of Confederate forces.

In *The Great American Myth*, historian George S. Bryan draws a picture of Booth, baffled in his futile efforts to save a South on the brink of defeat. April came and his plan was in tatters. His accomplices had lost enthusiasm for the enterprise; Arnold had openly threatened to pull out. In the meantime, General Grant, convinced that the South was defeated, had revoked the policy of not exchanging prisoners. So while Booth was planning his grand scheme to abduct the president as a hostage for Southern troops, thousands of those troops were already on their way home. Then Richmond fell, followed by the surrender of Lee's army. While Washington celebrated during the week of April 10, Booth, all of his grand patriotic ambitions dashed, was to be found in the capital's drinking spots, drowning himself and his bitter disappointment in brandy. He must have sharply felt that the brass ring of heroism was slipping from his grasp. The would-be hero needed to take action fast.

Under circumstances like these, it is hard to know when Booth formed the resolve to kill Lincoln. But it seems clear that he had assassination on

Standing on the steps of the newly completed U.S. Capitol on March 4, 1865, Lincoln calls for a "just and lasting" peace between the North and the South.

his mind by the evening of Tuesday, April 11. That evening, the capital's revelry was in full swing. A large crowd gathered in front of the White House. Bands were playing, while fireworks were lighting up the city. The people shouted for Lincoln. He appeared finally on the balcony and delivered an impromptu address—once again stressing his hope for reconciliation with the South. But when he stated his hope that the right to vote would be extended to blacks, one member of the audience turned to his tall, hulking companion and said, "That is the last speech he will ever make." The speaker was Booth; his companion was Paine. The president's fate was sealed.

On Thursday, April 13, Booth began to form the details of his plot. The rumor mill had it that General Grant and his family had that morning checked into the Willard House. Booth knew that the president's habit was to show off visiting dignitaries by taking them to the theater. He immediately checked the playbills. Ford's was showing *Our American Cousin,* but that play had made the circuit many times. So sure was Booth that the president would take Grant to the opening night of *Aladdin* at Grover's Theatre that he reserved for himself a box—the one right next to the president's!

A Fatal Coincidence

On the morning of April 14, Booth sauntered over to Ford's to see if he had any mail; he often used the theater as a mailing address when he was in town. His visit to the theater office that morning was a fatal coincidence for the president. As he glanced over his mail, Booth overheard Harry Ford, the manager, telling a stage carpenter that the Lincolns would be attending the play that evening. Booth learned that the president would be at Ford's, not Grover's.

Booth spent the next hours in a fever of activity. He reassembled his henchmen, arranged for horses, and generally scurried about town. At 2:30 in the afternoon he returned to his room at the National Hotel and changed into a smart riding outfit, including a new pair of spurs—the same that would later come close to foiling his escape as he leapt to the stage at Ford's. Later, he met with Mary Surratt, entrusting her with the package containing the gun that she delivered to a man named John Lloyd at his tavern in Surrattsville. At the nearby Herndon House, he met with Paine to steel him for the task of killing General Grant, who as far as Booth knew would be in the president's box. He dropped in at the Kirkwood House to rally Atzerodt, but when told that Atzerodt was not in, he took the puzzling step of leaving a message on a card for Vice President Johnson: "Don't wish to disturb you. Are you at home?" From the Kirkwood House, he went to

"Inspired by patriotic impulse and believing he was ridding the world of a monster, his name will be inscribed on the roll of true-hearted patriots."
Galveston (Texas) *Daily News*

"[The assassination was] the final insane act of a man whose twenty-six years of life had been weak and futile, who was a second-rater in his own profession, and who wanted to win the glaring floodlight of notoriety."
Historian Emanuel Hertz

Ford's to make final preparations. These included hiding the piece of wood he used to jam shut the door to the upstairs corridor leading to the president's box.

Booth returned to his hotel to dine and to arm himself with the derringer and dagger he would use later. At 8:00 he met for the last time with Paine, Atzerodt, and Herold. He unfolded his revised plan: Late in the afternoon he had seen the Grants leaving the city, so Paine, with Herold's help, was now to kill Secretary Seward, while Atzerodt was to kill the vice president. The killings were all to take place at 10:15. The conspirators were then to meet at the Navy Yard Bridge, enabling them to escape from Washington and head for the safety of the South.

By the time the conspirators' meeting ended, President and Mrs. Lincoln were in their seats watching *Our American Cousin.*

Booth Remains a Puzzle

To ask why John Wilkes Booth assassinated the president of the United States is to ask an unanswerable question. Historians have tried to understand, yet they remain frustrated by the shortcomings of the usual explanations. Was it "simple" insanity? The theories seem farfetched. The need for enduring fame? He was already a stage star, known and adored by thousands. A spy mission? The records that would answer this question are destroyed. His fanatical allegiance to the Southern cause? Booth rarely showed interest in political issues like slavery or states' rights. Frustration at his botched attempts at heroism? Then why were Seward, Grant, and Johnson part of the plan?

Furthermore, when historians examine the record of the events of April 14, 1865, and the weeks that followed, they see not a tidy narrative in which events follow causes in logical and explainable ways. Rather, they see discrepancies, unan-

David C. Herold was an avid hunter who knew the swampy country of lower Maryland. Herold served as a guide to Booth during the assassin's escape from federal forces.

Booth used this derringer to assassinate Lincoln.

swered questions, altered testimony, and bizarre co-incidences—all leading to the possible conclusion that Booth was not even the principal conspirator, but a tool in the hands of others. These historians ask, "Was the president betrayed by people he trusted? How could a twenty-six-year-old actor murder the president of the United States?"

They begin by asking why, as Booth stealthily crept toward the president's box armed with pistol and dagger, no one challenged him, no one stopped him.

Three

Evidence of a Conspiracy: Why Was the President Unprotected?

On the evening of April 14, 1865, President Abraham Lincoln sat in the presidential box at Ford's Theatre with no protection. Major Rathbone, who was in the box with him, was unarmed. John F. Parker, the police officer assigned the task of guarding the president, was not at his post. No Secret Service agents were in the theater, and no guards were posted around the building or at any of its doors. Theodore Roscoe sums up the situation:

> Under the circumstances—the curtain coming down on a savage civil war; Washington seething with excitement; the District infested with enemy parolees, spies, and saboteurs, some of whom were known to be nesting within a stone's throw of the Tenth Street playhouse—under these circumstances, the situation at Ford's Theatre seems incredible. Lincoln was exposed in the stage box like someone placed in a chair before the target of a rifle range.

The word "incredible" comes to mind for other reasons. Since his election in 1860, Lincoln had been the object of countless death threats. Even before he had taken office, he had been denounced in the press in cities throughout the South. Many people publicly admitted that they hated the president-elect because of his pledge to oppose the secession

(opposite page) Citizens pose beside the funeral train that carried the body of the slain president.

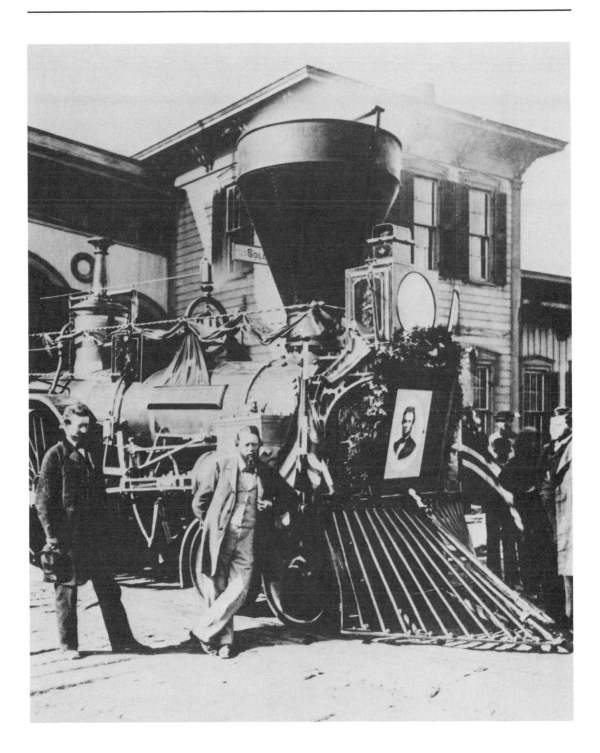

Slaves work a Southern plantation. Lincoln's pledge to oppose the secession of the Southern states over the issue of slavery caused many people to publicly admit their hatred of him.

of the Southern states over the slavery issue.

An early plot against Lincoln was exposed just before his journey from his home in Illinois to Washington to take office in February 1861. His close friend, Ward Lamon, caught word of a plan to kill Lincoln on his train. The head of the railroad hired Allan Pinkerton, the famous detective, to investigate. Pinkerton uncovered a plot among groups of fanatics who had drawn lots to decide who would kill the new president on his way through Baltimore. On the basis of this information, the president's train schedule was changed, and he passed safely through Baltimore under secret guard.

Plots like this were common throughout Lincoln's presidency:

• Pro-slavery forces in the South and anti-Lincoln "Copperheads" in the North vowed repeatedly to kill the president.

• A woman with smallpox, dressed as a widow,

approached the president and tried to infect him by kissing him.

• In 1864, a New York newspaper printed a letter describing an elaborate plot to kidnap the president.

• Union spies uncovered the activities of Thomas N. Conrad, a Confederate agent, whose plan to abduct Lincoln and carry him to Richmond bore a remarkable likeness to Booth's kidnap plot.

• In April 1864, a sniper shot at the president on the road near the Soldiers' Home in Washington. The hole in the president's characteristic "stove-pipe" hat was proof of the near miss.

• In December 1864, a newspaper in Selma, Alabama, printed a notice from "X" offering to kill Lincoln, Seward, and Johnson for one million dollars.

• On April 5, 1865, while the president was on a ship anchored outside Richmond, Union forces in the area captured and brought on board a Confederate agent. This agent claimed to be on a mission "aimed at the head of the Yankee government."

This was the atmosphere in April 1865 as the president sat with *no* armed protection in his box at Ford's.

Did the Authorities Ignore Information?

Today, highly trained Secret Service agents take elaborate measures to protect the president from harm. Accustomed as we are to seeing the president from behind walls of guards, the sight of Abraham Lincoln strolling by himself to, say, the War Department would be astonishing.

Yet Lincoln frequently went out without protection. Before Lincoln, no American president had ever been assassinated. Ward Lamon expressed the faith of many Americans when he wrote: "The crime of assassination was so abhorrent to the genius of . . . civilization, so foreign to the practice of our republican institutions, that little danger was apprehended." These words were written by a person who always seemed more anxious than anyone for the president's safety. They suggest how utterly unprepared the nation was for the calamity that occurred.

The responsibility for Lincoln's safety fell primarily to two men. One was Edwin M. Stanton, who as secretary of war had at his command all of the United States military. Stanton is one of the most intriguing figures in Lincoln's administration. He often acted like a stern dictator; biographers used words like "cunning" and "devious" to describe him. He had often expressed dislike for Lincoln, calling him a "long-legged ape," an "imbecile," and a "giraffe." Lincoln was aware of these gibes, yet he trusted Stanton.

Working closely with Stanton was Col. Lafayette C. Baker, who renamed the National Detective Police the National Secret Service. During the war, Baker had gathered his own army of two thousand agents, making him a powerful figure in Washington. Their mission was counterespionage—to spy on Confederate agents operating in the capital and other cities in the North. Stanton and Baker had generally managed to provide escorts for the president, but their efforts were haphazard at best.

Threats from Crackpots

Why did neither of these men take steps to protect the president while he was at Ford's? Historian Thomas Turner points out that many of the threats against Lincoln were from anonymous crackpots and that many had been false alarms. Stanton and Baker could not possibly have taken seriously every plot—and the rumor of every plot—against Lincoln. More importantly, many people believed that Lincoln was no longer in any real danger. The Civil War was over. Though the South lay in ruins, Lincoln wanted to follow a policy of peaceful reconstruction. So it seemed he should no longer have had to fear

Secretary of War Edwin M. Stanton disliked Lincoln. He called him a "long-legged ape," an "imbecile," and a "giraffe." Did Stanton participate in the conspiracy to kill the president?

plots directed by the South. Senator Orville Browning stated this view in his diary on the night of the assassination: "It seemed to me that the people in rebellion had many reasons for desiring the continuance of his life—none to wish his death."

Theodore Roscoe disputes both of these views. He says Stanton and Baker had little reason to assume that the danger to the president had passed. Rebel troops were still resisting in places like the Carolinas, Tennessee, Alabama, Texas, and even as close as Virginia. While fighting continued, the danger to the Union president was real. Further, the two men had often voiced fear for the president's safety. Baker's large army of spies had run down scores of Confederate agents, both in Washington's drawing rooms and in the Maryland swamps. How did it miss the band of conspirators operating out of a boarding house *eight blocks from the White House*?

A Brewing Conspiracy

This question takes on more urgency because of specific information authorities had about Booth and his cronies. Osborn Oldroyd was one of the earliest investigators to draw attention to the source of this information, a minor character named Louis J. Weichmann. Weichmann would later become a key government witness against Mary Surratt. In the months before the assassination, he was one of the lodgers at her boarding house at 541 H Street. He was with her on her trip to Surrattsville, when she delivered the package containing the gun to John Lloyd.

According to Oldroyd, Weichmann, who worked for the government, told Capt. D.H.L. Gleason, a friend who worked in the War Department, that a conspiracy to abduct the president was brewing among Weichmann's fellow boarders. This occurred sometime in March, but Weichmann and Gleason decided not to do anything with the information until something further happened—whatever they

"It is astonishing that the Government did not find out these things [assassination threats] and put a stop to them."

Louis J. Weichmann, lodger at Surratt's boarding house

"In cases where there seemed a ground for inquiry it was made, as carefully as possible . . . but always without substantial result. Warnings that appeared to be most definite, when they came to be examined proved too vague and confused for further attention."

John Nicolay and John Hay, Lincoln's secretaries

thought that something might be.

Historian Otto Eisenschiml tells a somewhat different version of this story. He puts the date of Weichmann's conversation with Gleason as February 20. More important, he emphasizes that Weichmann was specific, reporting secret conversations between Booth and Mary Surratt, John Surratt's secret trips into Maryland, and an atmosphere of furtive comings and goings among an assortment of Confederate spies. Most important, Eisenschiml believes that Gleason did not sit on this information. Rather, he passed it on to Stanton through the appropriate chain of command. In the meantime, Weichmann had offered similar information to another army officer, and evidence shows that he also notified his superiors. After the assassination, Stanton and Baker almost immediately ordered the arrest of the boarding house conspirators, suggesting that Weichmann's report had reached them.

Roscoe asks why the War Department and Secret Service failed to act on this information: "Here was a house openly 'Secesh' [that is, in favor of secession], a family that entertained a Confederate spy, a mysterious gang of men, reportedly armed. . . . Nothing was done."

Mary Surratt owned the boardinghouse where Booth and others met to discuss their plans.

Where Was the President's Bodyguard?

The legend has grown up around Lincoln that he refused protection. He did not want guards separating him from the people who wanted to talk with him: "It would never do for a President to have guards with drawn sabers at his door, as if he fancied he were . . . an emperor." His friends and advisers were troubled by his willingness to go out in public by himself. But on the afternoon of April 14, at least, Lincoln went out of his way to get protection for his trip to the theater.

After his carriage ride with Mrs. Lincoln, the president walked over to the War Department. He hoped to find word that Johnston had surrendered to

Union forces. While there, he took the opportunity to ask Stanton for the services of Maj. Thomas T. Eckert, a tall, muscular War Department officer Lincoln thought would be equal to the task of protecting him.

Stanton refused.

According to David H. Bates, a War Department employee who overheard the conversation, Stanton claimed that Eckert had "important" work to do that evening. Not satisfied with the secretary's brusque refusal of his request, Lincoln ambled into the telegraph room, which Eckert supervised, and put the question to the major himself. Eckert confirmed what Stanton had said, insisting that he had vital work to do in the telegraph room that evening.

Unnecessary Danger

Historian William Hanchett expresses the general interpretation of Stanton's decision: that he refused Lincoln because he disapproved of the president's theater-going, fearing that it put him in unnecessary danger. Stanton thought that to agree to the president's request would be to encourage a foolhardy course of action. In Bates's words, Stanton was "unwilling to encourage the theater project" and thought that denying Lincoln the guard he wanted would keep him at home.

Eisenschiml, however, sees this incident in a different light. He notes first that just a few days later, Stanton gave a version of his "final interview" with Lincoln that differed in every particular from the version Bates reported. Second, Eisenschiml notes that in testimony to Congress in 1868, Stanton twice said that the last time he saw Lincoln was not on April 14, but earlier in the week. Third, Eisenschiml examined the cables that came into the telegraph room that evening—the evening Eckert had "important" work to do. In fact, only a handful of cables arrived. The one that was for Lincoln was sent by messenger to the White House, rather than to Ford's.

Hours before he went to the theater, Lincoln asked Secretary of War Stanton to appoint Maj. Thomas T. Eckert to be his bodyguard for the occasion. Stanton refused, saying Eckert had "important" work to do that evening.

This suggests that Eckert, who knew where the president could be found, was not even on duty.

The Stanton-Eckert incident raises another question. Why did General Grant turn down the president's invitation to the theater? At first he had accepted, and Washington's afternoon newspapers were announcing that he would be at Ford's with the Lincolns. Many people would attend the play just to catch a glimpse of the Civil War hero. It seems unlikely that Grant would back out of the engagement without a good reason. A high-ranking army officer does not lightly turn down a "request" from his commander-in-chief, let alone accept it, then change his mind. And yet, that is just what Grant seems to have done.

Writer Jim Bishop accepts the explanation Grant

Some historians believe Grant declined Lincoln's invitation to the theater because Grant's wife Julia (standing behind him) had recently quarreled with Lincoln's wife Mary.

gave for this unusual action: that he wanted to take the 6:00 P.M. train to Philadelphia, then on to New Jersey, to visit his children. Biographers Dorothy Kunhardt and Philip Kunhardt, on the other hand, stress the humiliating public quarrel that Julia Grant, the general's wife, had recently had with Mary Lincoln. Grant backed out, in their view, because he had little desire to spend a social evening with Mrs. Lincoln.

Roscoe and Eisenschiml find both of these explanations hard to accept. Grant had only recently seen his children. The train schedules were such that the Grants had to travel all night. The train leaving the next morning, though, would have put them in New Jersey only a few hours later, at far less trouble. Both writers hint at a darker explanation: that someone played on the general's dislike of public appearances to get him out of the way. If Grant had been in the box at Ford's, the theater and the surrounding streets and alleys would have been packed with military men. The general's aides would have formed a solid barrier around the president. But with Grant on a train headed north, the president would be more vulnerable—and an assassin could easily escape. Stanton knew that Grant had turned down Lincoln's invitation. Why, then, did he refuse the president the bodyguard he asked for?

Where Was John Parker?

At 4:00 in the afternoon of April 14, John F. Parker, a member of the city police force, was due to arrive at the White House to take over for William Crook as the president's bodyguard. He showed up at 7:00—a full three hours late.

Parker's tardiness was no surprise. Since he had joined the force in 1861, his record had been dismal. He was regularly reprimanded for drunkenness, disrespect, and neglect of duty. His known associates included many of the city's petty criminals, barflies, and streetwalkers.

"[Stanton was] a superbly effective secretary of war, and Lincoln's true friend."
Historian William Hanchett

"Brusque, insolent, cruel, Stanton was without doubt the most unpopular member of Lincoln's administration."
Historian Otto Eisenschiml

On the night of his death, Lincoln sat in an upholstered rocking chair on the far left side of the president's box. He was twelve feet above the stage, and most of the audience could not see him.

This man was given the responsibility of guarding the president of the United States during a public appearance.

Every historian of the Lincoln assassination asks why Parker was even a member of the White House detail. His background, training, and record did not entitle him to a promotion out of the ranks of the police department. And yet he owed his position, at least in part, to Mary Lincoln. On April 3, less than two weeks before her husband was murdered, Mrs. Lincoln wrote the following note to a local official, asking him to exempt Parker from the military draft:

> This is to certify that John F. Parker, a member of the Metropolitan Police has been detailed for duty at the Executive Mansion by order of,
>
> Mrs. Lincoln

Curiously, no one ever investigated what prompted Mrs. Lincoln to shield Parker from the draft. Why she did so has never been made clear. For Roscoe, this curious gap in the records suggests that a "veil of censorship" was thrown over the relationship between Parker and the president's wife. In any event, it was Parker who was immediately responsible for the safety of Abraham Lincoln as the president sat watching *Our American Cousin* just after 10:00 on the evening of April 14.

After arriving at the White House, Parker was sent on to Ford's where he was to wait for the Lincoln party. They arrived at 8:30, and when the play resumed at 8:45, Parker presumably sat just outside the presidential box, where he would be unable to see any of the action onstage. William Crook, Lincoln's bodyguard earlier in the day, assumes that Parker left his post to find a better seat in the balcony. Witnesses say they saw Booth stop and hand a card to someone in the balcony as he made his way to the president's box. But no evidence proves it was Parker. Later writers like James O. Hall suggest that the kindly Lincoln may have dismissed Parker, wanting to relieve the officer of a duty the president saw as unnecessary. A very different story is told by Francis Burns, the driver of Lincoln's carriage waiting outside Ford's. His account was that he and Parker, along with Charles Forbes, the president's footman, went for a drink in the tavern next door, the same one Booth went into some time between 9:30 and 10:00. In either event, Parker was not at his post at the critical time, and he did not reappear until 6:00 the next morning.

Neglect of Duty

In the aftermath of the assassination, Parker was charged with "neglect of duty." One assumes that he would have paid the severest of penalties. In fact, no record of the official hearing exists, and on June 3, 1865, the charge was dropped. Incredibly, Parker served as a member of the White House detail for another month, and as a member of the police force for three years. Roscoe believes that Parker was not thoroughly investigated because officials wanted to protect Mrs. Lincoln. Eisenschiml

"That Secretary of War Stanton wanted to get rid of Lincoln . . . is not worth an argument."

Historian Emanuel Hertz

"If the conspirators were fairly tried and justly convicted—if Stanton's War Department had clean hands—then *why the secrecy?*"

Writer Theodore Roscoe, referring to the sealed records

draws a more intriguing conclusion. He points out that Parker's official record after the assassination improved dramatically, but that he was dismissed in 1868 for a fairly minor offense just weeks after Stanton left public service. Eisenschiml asks whether Stanton for some unknown reason had been using his position to protect Parker.

How Did It Happen?

How could an armed assassin step to within two feet of the president of the United States in a theater filled with over 1,500 people? How could he fire a gun point-blank at the president without being stopped or challenged?

The traditional explanation is that no one could have foreseen the tragic events that occurred in those fatal minutes after 10:00. Booth was able to carry out his mad plan because of an unlucky combination of circumstances, and because no one re-

How was Booth able to step within two feet of the president of the United States in a theater filled with over 1,500 people and fire a gun at point-blank range? Was it a conspiracy?

ally believed the president was in danger.

Yet some historians feel that there has to be another explanation. These historians remain troubled by a number of questions:

• How could the president be allowed to sit in a theater without protection when he had been the object of many threats and when actual attempts had been made to kidnap and assassinate him? Why did officials fail to act on Weichmann's information?

• Why did Stanton refuse to assign to the president an apparently capable bodyguard, especially since he knew that General Grant would not be with the Lincolns? Did he lie to the president when he said that Eckert had important work to do that evening? Did he forget, or was he lying, when he said later that the last time he had seen Lincoln was on April 13?

• Why did General Grant violate the dictates of official good manners by suddenly declining his commander-in-chief's invitation to the theater?

• Why was the nation's most important elected official under the guard of the city's most unreliable police officer? Where was that officer at the moment when Booth fired the fatal shot? Why was he never punished for his tragic neglect of duty?

To historians who ask these questions, the facts form a pattern. This pattern strongly suggests that Lincoln's death might not have been the result of the actions of a lone gunman. They suggest that Abraham Lincoln was the victim of a larger conspiracy.

If there is a pattern, it did not end on the morning of April 15. It continued during the days and weeks following the assassination, ending with one of the most infamous trials in the annals of American justice.

"That Parker seriously failed in his duty during the performance of *Our American Cousin* is a matter beyond dispute."
Historian Otto Eisenschiml

"The president dismissed [Parker] and told him to take a seat and enjoy the play."
Historian James O. Hall

Four

Evidence of a Conspiracy: Bringing the Accused to Justice

The conspiracy trial that opened on May 9, 1865, was the last step in the government's effort to bring those accused of Lincoln's murder to justice. Whether the trial was a fair one or not has long been debated. The steps leading to the trial—those that had to do with the pursuit and capture of the conspirators—have been the source of many questions as well. Some of these questions bear on events that took place during Lincoln's final hours.

The Search for the Assassin

The hunt for John Wilkes Booth began within minutes. In the audience at Ford's was Maj. Almarin C. Richards, superintendent of the Metropolitan Police Force. Richards recognized Booth and sprang into action. He rushed to police headquarters nearby and ordered detectives to comb the area for Booth. Within the hour, they had descended on the National Hotel, where Booth had been staying. They also began to stake out the Surratt boardinghouse on H Street. By midnight, Richards was sure of the identity of the killer. In the meantime, he had taken a statement from John Fletcher, a stable keeper who had pursued David Herold after Herold stole one of his horses. In this way, Richards was

(opposite page) Lafayette Baker (seated), his cousin Lt. Luther Baker (left), and Lt. Col. Everton Conger plan the capture of Booth. They later found Booth and Herold inside a tobacco barn sixty miles south of Ford's Theatre.

also sure of the assassin's escape route—the Navy Yard Bridge.

The events of the next few hours were typical of the confusion and disorder that would mark the effort to find Booth. Almost immediately, the police and assorted military units began to compete rather than cooperate. Richards, for example, wanted to mount a police posse that would cross the Navy Yard Bridge and head south into Maryland. He approached Gen. Christopher Augur, the provost marshal in Washington (that is, the head of the military police), asking for cavalry horses. Augur refused. Both Roscoe and Eisenschiml believe that had Augur granted the chief's request—and there were plenty of horses at hand—Booth would have been in custody by morning. As it was, patrols were not sent until several hours later, giving Booth and Herold ample time to make their escape.

Augur's unexplained foot-dragging did not stop there. Fletcher was brought forward to tell his story to Augur himself. Once again, Augur failed to take action. Then Captain Gleason, the officer to whom Louis Weichmann had told his story about the conspiracy brewing on H Street, asked Augur for permission to lead a patrol south into Maryland. He knew that Port Tobacco was the destination of the kidnap plot. Like Richards, Gleason was refused. Oldroyd suggests that this bungling was the outcome of typical government red tape. But Eisenschiml offers the possibility that Augur refused to take decisive action under orders from higher up.

The Role of Secretary Stanton

Some of Stanton's decisions that night seem peculiar as well. Operating from a room near the dying president, the war secretary firmly seized the reins of government. Throughout the long night, he sat at the center of a frenzy of activity, making decisions and issuing orders. Some historians, like Thomas Turner, give him high marks for acting responsibly under trying conditions. But Navy Secretary Gideon Welles was less tolerant. He called Stanton's decisions that night "exceedingly repugnant." Roscoe characterizes many of Stanton's decisions as "legally insupportable"—like ordering the arrest of all the actors at Ford's. Bishop writes, "For . . . eight hours, the United States was run by a dictator."

Puzzling Orders

Stanton's first puzzling decision was really one he failed to make—that of closing the bridges leading from the capital. Situated where the Potomac and Anacostia rivers meet, Washington, D.C., is almost an island. To avoid using a bridge, Booth would have had to flee to the Union north, right into enemy territory. At 11:30, though, Stanton telegraphed a cavalry station *north* of the city, informing those on duty that "the assassins are supposed to have escaped toward Maryland." But since Maryland surrounds Washington on three sides, Stanton's message seems of little use. As the night wore on, Stanton sent a series of wires to military and police authorities, ordering bridges closed and roadblocks

"On the 19th of April . . . it was not positively known who had assassinated the President."

Col. Harry Burnet, assistant judge advocate at the trial

"John Wilkes Booth has shot the president!"

James C. Ferguson, in Ford's audience

After Lincoln was shot, Secretary of War Stanton ordered that all of Washington's avenues of escape be sealed—except for the Navy Yard Bridge, the route that Booth took.

Dr. Samuel Mudd was sentenced to hard labor for treating Booth's broken leg. Mudd claimed that he had not known who his patient was, even though the two had previously met.

set up. He thus sealed the capital off on all sides and closed off all avenues of escape—except the Navy Yard Bridge, the escape route Booth took and the *only* one leading directly south to the safety of the Confederacy. Why did Stanton not close off this bridge first?

Another mystery is Stanton's failure to identify Booth as the assassin. His first official statement about the tragedy was a telegram sent to Gen. John Dix in New York. As New York's military commandant, Dix would be responsible for informing the national news services of the shooting, and thus alerting the public to the killer's identity.

Sent at 2:15 A.M., the telegram gave Dix a detailed summary of the violent events four hours earlier. But the telegram did not mention Booth. Bishop points out that the news services already knew that Booth was the chief suspect. But when they saw Stanton's telegram—the first official word they had seen—they decided to omit Booth's name from their early morning stories. Not until after 3:00 A.M. did Stanton send a second telegram to Dix, this time naming Booth—too late for the early editions of the papers.

Pursuit and Capture

Bishop attributes the second telegram to a change of mind. Stanton "had begun with the notion that Washington was seething with assassins and arsonists; that a reign of terror had overtaken the city and death was to overtake many people before dawn." He was less interested, then, in finding Booth than in protecting the city and the government. But by 3:00, he believed that the violence was the work of at most a handful of people. Now he could turn his energy to their pursuit and capture. Eisenschiml, however, takes a different view. He emphasizes that the assassination reports in the early editions of even the local papers were vague. To Eisenschiml, this vagueness, added to the delay in publicly identifying Booth, suggests that information about the assassin and his flight was for some reason, and by someone, purposefully withheld.

Booth in Flight

Early in the morning of Saturday, April 15, Booth and David Herold reached the Maryland home of Dr. Samuel Mudd. Roused from his bed while it was still dark, Mudd tended to Booth's broken leg. His name will live in history as that of the man who aided the fugitive killer of Abraham Lincoln. (The expression that someone's "name is Mudd"—that is, the person is to be scorned—is probably a reference to the doctor, not to the word "mud.")

The extent of Mudd's participation in the conspiracy has been unclear from the start. Mudd later insisted that he did not know who his patient was even though he had previously been acquainted with Booth. He claimed that Booth's companion—Herold—told him that the injured man was a "Mr. Tyson." He further claimed that the patient kept his muffled face turned away. And of course, word of the assassination had not yet spread. When it did, Mudd himself asked his pro-Union brother to notify the authorities of the suspicious characters who had intruded into his home that morning.

But Mudd was a known Southern sympathizer. What damaged his believability was that he gave the fugitives directions through area swamps to the plantation of Samuel Cox, a Southern agent whose home was part of the Confederate Underground. Here, Cox and Thomas Jones fed and sheltered the fugitives for six full days. Cox and Jones were later arrested, but for reasons that may never be clear, they were released. But Mudd, who harbored the fugitives for a few hours before word of the assassination spread, was arrested, tried, convicted, and sentenced to hard labor. To this day, his descendants

Ned Spangler, a stagehand at Ford's Theatre, was sentenced to life imprisonment for his role in the assassination. Spangler waited with Booth's horse behind the theater while Booth was inside.

The upper right-hand window marks the room that Booth and Herold occupied at Mudd's house.

have been trying to clear his name.

By April 19, all of the conspirators except Booth, Herold, and John Surratt were in custody. Michael O'Laughlin, Sam Arnold, and Ned Spangler were taken on Monday, April 17. Late that evening, detectives closed on Mary Surratt's boarding house and arrested her. While they were inside, the doorbell sounded, and when one of the detectives answered it, there stood Louis Paine. Dr. Mudd was taken on April 18. Atzerodt was cornered and seized by a cavalry detachment in Maryland on April 19.

But the leading figure was still at large, and Stanton was growing impatient. So on Thursday, April 20, he issued posters offering rewards totaling $100,000—an immense sum of money in 1865—for the capture of Booth, Herold, and Surratt. In the meantime, he had ordered Lafayette Baker to lead the search.

The combination of Baker and the reward money would prove too much for Booth. Baker wanted the money, and he went after it with astonishing zeal. During his investigation he arrested and held hundreds of suspects. No lead was too flimsy. Then, he summoned to his office two of his men. One was Lt. Luther Baker, his cousin; the other was his top investigator, Lt. Col. Everton Conger. To their surprise, he announced that he knew where the fugitives were.

Later, Baker claimed that he picked up their scent from one of his agents. In fact—at least according to Roscoe—evidence shows that Baker learned the whereabouts of the fugitives from a Dr. James Coombe, who had spotted them on the Cox plantation. Coombe, feeling that Baker was interested only in the reward money, passed his information directly to the War Department. How Baker got hold of it remains unclear. What's more, surviving telegrams suggest that Baker may have intentionally thwarted the efforts of another cavalry troop already on Booth's trail. Did he fear that he would lose his claim to the reward?

The Death of John Wilkes Booth

Early on the morning of April 26, a cavalry troop dispatched by Baker and led by the young Lieutenant Colonel Conger, Lieutenant Baker, and Lt. Edward Doherty crept through the Virginia darkness to surround the tobacco barn of Richard Garrett, sixty miles south of Ford's Theatre. Inside were Booth and Herold. When Conger threatened to torch the barn, Herold surrendered and was taken into custody. Booth, however, had vowed never to be taken alive, and when he refused to come out, Conger set fire to the barn. As the barn's interior began to glow with flames, the troops could see the actor moving about inside. He then appeared in an

"Every effort that ingenuity, excited by fervor, can make, is being put forth by all the proper authorities to capture or trace the assassins."
Philadelphia *Evening Star*

"By now a fog of confusion settled on the nation's military headquarters. It slowed the manhunt, obscured the assassin's trail, and did everything to abet an escape."
Writer Theodore Roscoe

open doorway. Suddenly a shot rang out, and Booth fell forward. He was dragged from the burning barn and died a few hours later—of a gunshot wound in nearly the same spot as the slain president's.

The Voice of God

Many of the details surrounding Booth's death have remained shrouded in mystery. The cavalry was under the strictest orders from the War Department to take Booth alive. Doherty repeatedly told the men to hold their fire. Stepping forward to take credit—or blame—for the shooting was Sgt. Boston Corbett, who claimed that the voice of God told him to fire the shot. Despite the fact that Booth's death ended any chance the nation would have to understand the full extent of the conspiracy, Corbett was never punished for this clear violation of orders. Though arrested, he was released by Stanton. Why Stanton, a stern disciplinarian, would tolerate such a breach of duty is a mystery. Though Corbett and John Parker never met, they had something in common—the unexplained forbearance of Stanton.

Possibly, Stanton knew that Corbett was not guilty. None of Corbett's fellow troopers witnessed the shot, and many of them scoffed at his bizarre claim. In later testimony, Conger stated that Booth had committed suicide with a pistol he was holding just before he fell. Lieutenant Baker, on the other hand, believed that *Conger* fired the shot, and raised the question of whether Conger had secret orders to kill Booth to prevent him from telling all he knew about who was behind the assassination. Historian David DeWitt points out that officials could easily have figured out which gun fired the shot, but that they simply failed to do so.

That Sgt. Boston Corbett killed John Wilkes Booth is a piece of American folklore that has never been proven, or disproven.

Two further mysteries surround Booth's death. Sensationalized versions of the assassination drama have suggested that Booth made good his escape and died years later—in Europe, Canada, California, and a variety of other places. A notorious circus show claimed to have Booth's body on display. While many of the circumstances of Booth's death remain obscure, no serious historian of the assassination doubts that it was John Wilkes Booth who was shot in Garrett's barn. Roscoe and others, though, raise questions about whether his body was in the coffin hurriedly buried in Washington's Old Arsenal Penitentiary.

Mystery also surrounds the fate of Booth's diary. After Booth's death, Everton Conger rushed off to Colonel Baker's office, bearing the assassin's diary. The two then went to Stanton, who took charge of the diary. Stanton in turn entrusted it to Major Eckert, who locked it in a War Department safe.

This painting depicts the shooting of Booth and the capture of Herold at Garrett's farm, eleven days after Lincoln's death.

During President Andrew Johnson's impeachment trial in 1867, Booth's diary was brought to light. Eighteen pages—covering the days just before the assassination—had been cut out of the diary. What was in those pages?

Strangely, the diary was never mentioned in the conspiracy trial and was not brought to light until the impeachment trial of Andrew Johnson in 1867. Then it was discovered that eighteen pages had been cut out—the pages covering the days just before the assassination. Since then, various people have claimed to have the missing pages, or to have seen and read them. None of these claims has been verified. The mysterious handling of Booth's diary silenced the assassin's voice. Who cut out the missing pages? Why? What was in those pages?

The Conspiracy Trial

With Booth dead and all of the conspirators except John Surratt in custody, government officials led by Stanton wanted quick justice. On May 9,

1865, the eight prisoners—Louis Paine, George Atzerodt, David Herold, Samuel Mudd, Michael O'Laughlin, Samuel Arnold, Ned Spangler, and Mary Surratt—were led into a makeshift courtroom in the Old Arsenal Penitentiary in Washington. All except Mary Surratt were in chains, and throughout their captivity all had been forced to wear thick padded hoods over their heads. Roscoe believes that in this way the prisoners were "cruelly tortured" with a view to forcing confessions from them. Eisenschiml, however, hints that the prisoners were hooded and held in solitary confinement to prevent them from telling anyone all that they knew about the assassination.

Public Enemies

The trial sparked controversy even before it began. The accused were civilians, so ordinarily they would have been tried in a civilian court. Their rights would then have been protected by all of the rules that govern such trials. Stanton, however, insisted that the trial be conducted by a military commission. The new president, Andrew Johnson, submitted the question to his attorney general, James Speed. Speed concluded that because the conspirators were "public enemies" and because the nation had still been at war when they committed the crime, they "ought to be tried before a military tribunal." On May 1, Johnson ordered that "nine competent military officers" be appointed to conduct the trial. Prosecuting the government's case was Brig. Gen. Joseph Holt, head of the War Department's Bureau of Military Justice and an old friend of Stanton's.

A question still open today is why the trial was a military rather than a civilian one. Champ Clark summarizes the customary view: A military court was likely to be more severe in its treatment of guilty parties. Stanton wanted the punishment to be quick and harsh to prevent anti-South feeling from

Ex-Confederate soldier Michael O'Laughlin was Booth's school friend. O'Laughlin, Booth, and Samuel Arnold hatched the initial plot to kidnap Lincoln.

According to one witness at the military trial, Confederate president Jefferson Davis, pictured here, approved of the planned assassinations of Lincoln, Grant, Stanton, and other Union leaders.

growing in the North. Only in this way, Stanton believed, could the North peacefully reunite with the South. But if suspicions arose in the North that the accused were treated lightly, the attitude of the North would be poisoned by a desire for vengeance. So if the attorney general of the United States was convinced that a military trial was legal, Stanton was ready to proceed.

Many people, however, openly opposed the idea of a military trial. Newspapers such as the *New York Times* and the New York *Tribune* ran editorials arguing that trying civilians in a military court was unconstitutional. Others criticized the secrecy of military trials, wanting to know what the government had to hide. Turner, though, points out that opponents of the military trial assumed that a civilian trial would be fairer. That assumption, Turner says, might not have been true. The public was so inflamed against the prisoners that a fairer trial in a civilian court was unlikely. While the nature of the trial may have been illegal, in the end, Turner concludes, justice was served as well as it would have been in a civilian court.

Was the Conspiracy Trial Fairly Conducted?

Had the prisoners been tried fairly, no one would have been very concerned about the abstract question of military versus civilian trials. But historians are unanimous in their belief that the trial was not fair. The defendants were going to be found guilty—of that there was never any real doubt.

During the weeks between their capture in mid-April and the start of the trial in May, the prisoners were held in solitary confinement, with the hated hoods over their heads. They were never allowed to obtain defense lawyers. When the formal charges against them were read on May 9, they still had no lawyers. Even after lawyers were found, the defendants were never allowed to confer with them in private. Nearly all of the four hundred witnesses called over the next six weeks testified for the prosecution. Many of these witnesses were called by surprise; often they were dismissed before the defense attorneys were allowed to cross-examine them. The defendants were never allowed to speak on their own behalf. Objections raised by the defense were almost always overruled. One of the members of the commission was heard to say that he knew Mudd was guilty—because of the shape of the bumps on his head. Another openly accused Mary Surratt's lawyer of disloyalty to the Union. Witness after witness was coached on what to say, usually by Stanton. Later information revealed that many of these witnesses were imposters and that their testimony was pure fabrication.

Controversial Testimony

One of the most dramatic of these witnesses was Sanford Conover. Claiming to be a writer for the New York *Tribune*, Conover testified that he had become associated with the "Canadian Cabinet" in Montreal. There he had seen Booth strutting about, flourishing dispatches he had received from Jefferson Davis approving the assassination of Lincoln, Grant, Stanton, Seward, and other Union leaders. Conover's testimony had impact. It convinced both the commission and the public that the conspiracy extended to the Confederate leadership. But there was one catch: After the trial, officials discovered that Conover was really Charles Dunham, and that his testimony was entirely false. He spent ten years in prison for perjury.

The most controversial aspect of the trial concerned the guilt or innocence of Mary Surratt. Her supporters would later call her conviction and execution "judicial murder." Until the end, Surratt maintained that she was only a passive bystander—that she knew nothing of the intentions of her son, Booth, and the others. What doomed her, though, were four pieces of evidence. One was the testi-

"If Booth had not broken his leg, we would never have heard the name of Dr. Mudd."

Gen. Lew Wallace, member, military commission

"Your argument . . . did not convince me that the d___d rascal [Mudd] ought not to be hung."

J.M. Connell to Mudd's attorney, Thomas Ewing

mony of John Lloyd, the Surrattsville tavern keeper, which suggested that Mary Surratt knew the contents of the package she delivered to him. A second was her denial that her son John had ever taken trips into the South—a clearly untrue statement. The third was her denial that she recognized Paine when he appeared at her door on the night of her arrest.

But most damaging was the testimony of boarder Louis J. Weichmann, who described months of furtive movements and secret conversations involving the widow and the other conspirators. Shelton calls Weichmann "gossipy," and Turner calls Weichmann's long book about his role "self-serving," for Weichmann testified against Mary Surratt in exchange for not being tried himself as one of the conspirators. Nonetheless, the commission believed him, and Mary Surratt was hanged—this in spite of pleas for leniency from several members of the military court. In later years, Andrew Johnson vehemently denied ever seeing the petitions Brigadier General Holt and others claimed they submitted.

Dogged Determination

While historians agree that the trial was badly conducted, the question remains, why? The principal conspirator was dead. The guilt of Paine, Atzerodt, and Herold was easily established. Why was the government so determined to prosecute minor characters like Mary Surratt, Mudd, Spangler, Arnold, and O'Laughlin? Why did Stanton stay up until dawn, poring over lists of witnesses, determined to control the course and the outcome of the trial? Why, given this dogged determination, did he repeatedly refuse to take steps that would lead to the capture of John Surratt?

Historians agree that Stanton had political reasons for wanting to control the trial. For it must be recalled that the bill of charges read in court on May 9 named not only the eight defendants, but the

Louis Paine was sentenced to death for stabbing Secretary of State William Seward twice and for attacking Seward's son.

leaders of the Confederacy as well. In a real sense, the defendants were not on trial. They were already doomed. On trial was the South, and most of the government's witnesses gave testimony involving Davis and the Canadian Cabinet. Viewed in this light, the government's failure to call John Parker, Bessie Hale, Samuel Cox, or Thomas Jones is easily explained. These people might have had plenty to say. But none of what they had to say would have added to the government's "case" against the South.

But other historians argue that the conspiracy trial was staged—and staged for more sinister reasons. In their minds, the evidence points to the possibility that high-ranking officials in Lincoln's own administration were responsible for the president's death. Everything, from the mysterious disappearance of John Parker to the "silencing" of the accused, left behind the smell of a hideous conspiracy—inside the Union government.

"Would it have been inconvenient to anyone to have taken [Booth] with the power to speak?"

Beverley Tucker, member of the Canadian Cabinet

"Those who know [Booth] best, feel confident that he has committed suicide."

Gettysburg *Compiler*

Five

Who Was Responsible for Lincoln's Death?

Close inspection of the "facts" surrounding the assassination of Abraham Lincoln uncovers a web of coincidences, unexplained acts, and unanswered questions. A bodyguard is mysteriously gone from his post, and is never punished. An informant reveals a sinister plot hatching just blocks from the White House, and no action is taken. The president makes a simple request for a bodyguard from his war secretary, and is strangely turned down. The assassin flees from the scene of the crime unhindered, then later is gunned down by a soldier acting against orders. He keeps a record of his actions, and it disappears. His accomplices are captured and tried, but instead of being made to tell what happened, they are silenced, some by hanging. Any one of these and dozens of other mysteries would by themselves mean little. Taken together, say some historians, they point to an inescapable conclusion: Abraham Lincoln, the sixteenth president of the United States, was betrayed.

His death was the work not of a crazed gunman, but of powerful persons able to use their power to cover up their crime. In Roscoe's words, "The criminals responsible for Lincoln's death got away with murder."

During the nineteenth century, two conspiracy theories were widely believed. One, of course, was that Jefferson Davis and the Southern leadership were behind Lincoln's death. According to this view, Booth was an agent employed by the South to cut down the North's leader, paving the way for the South's final assault. This view was officially confirmed on May 2, 1865, when President Johnson, on Stanton's urging, signed a sensational proclamation naming the Southern "conspirators" and offering rewards for their capture. By "trying" Davis, Stanton gave added support to this belief. It seems puzzling, then, that after Davis was captured on May 10 in Georgia, Stanton voted to put him on trial for treason but not for the assassination.

The second theory was that Lincoln's death was the work of none other than the new president, Andrew Johnson. Of course, suspicion naturally fell on him because Lincoln's death made him president. Booth's mysterious note left in Johnson's box at the Kirkwood House on the afternoon of the assassination was never satisfactorily explained, and Johnson was never able to account for two hours of his time that night.

Peaceful Reconciliation

The fire of this suspicion was later fanned by some extreme members of Johnson's own Republican party. The so-called "Radical Republicans" were actually glad Lincoln was dead. They believed Johnson would treat the South more like conquered territory. They came quickly to resent Johnson's surprising efforts to carry out Lincoln's plans for peaceful reconciliation with the Rebel states. In 1867, these extremists tried to get Johnson out of office—without success—by impeaching him. One of their accusations, backed by testimony given by Lafayette Baker, was that he had been a Rebel spy. Their far more serious accusation was that he was behind the assassination. Judge Holt's accusation

Since Lincoln's death made Andrew Johnson president, some people believe Johnson was part of the conspiracy to kill Lincoln. Johnson was unable to account for two hours of his time on the night Lincoln was shot.

The April 15, 1865 edition of the *New York Herald* describes the events surrounding Lincoln's death. Do the events reveal that Lincoln was betrayed by men within his own administration?

that Johnson deliberately let Mary Surratt go to her death did not help the president—a president the public never forgave for attending Lincoln's second inauguration while drunk and who paid only the briefest of visits to the dying president's bedside.

Other theories made the rounds, too. Some people remained convinced that the source of the plot was Northern subversive organizations like the Knights of the Golden Circle, a "patriotic" society resembling the Know-Nothing Party Booth joined. Still others were persuaded that the conspiracy originated with the Catholic Church in Rome. The Surratts, Dr. Mudd, and Weichmann were Catholics, and the story was told that Booth died clutching a Catholic medal. In the twentieth century, the German Nazis spread the view that Booth was employed by prominent Jewish bankers opposed to Lincoln's economic policies. None of these theories has any support. But the way in which people could so easily believe them underscores the fact that many secrets were buried with Booth's body (if it was Booth's body!) under the Old Arsenal Penitentiary.

Before the twentieth century, Lincoln's assassination was never closely studied by professional historians. The hundreds of books and magazine ar-

Did William Seward, David Bates, Edward M. Stanton, and other members of Lincoln's cabinet know of the plot to kill the president?

Copyright, 1876 by Currier & Ives, N.Y.

GIDEON WELLES, Sec. of the Navy.   MONTGOMERY BLAIR, P.M. Gen'l   CALEB B. SMITH, Sec. of the Interior.

PRESIDENT LINCOLN.   SALMON P. CHASE, Sec. of the Treasury.   WILLIAM H. SEWARD, Sec. of State.   EDWARD BATES, Atty. Gen'l   EDWIN M. STANTON, Sec. of War.

PRESIDENT LINCOLN AND HIS CABINET.

IN COUNCIL, SEPT. 22ND 1862. ADOPTING THE EMANCIPATION PROCLAMATION, ISSUED JAN'Y. 1ST 1863.

ticles on the subject were written by the scores of people who were involved in the assassination and its aftermath. And because the War Department kept its official assassination records under lock and key until the 1930s, few attempts were made to piece the events together into a coherent story. Lincoln and his death had fast become legend, but serious historical studies were lacking.

During the 1930s, the government made these records available to the public for the first time. The result was a number of books examining the assassination not just as part of Lincoln's biography nor as part of the history of the Civil War but as a historical event in its own right.

Some of these books reach startling and controversial conclusions.

The Eisenschiml Theory

Preceding chapters have frequently mentioned the name of Otto Eisenschiml, an Austrian chemist and businessman who turned to the study of American history. In 1937, he published a book entitled *Why Was Lincoln Murdered?* In numerous articles over the next twenty-five years, until his death in 1963, he developed and defended his theory about the conspiracy that led to the tragedy at Ford's Theatre. Eisenschiml's book proved to be enormously influential with later writers on the assassination.

Eisenschiml says that the starting point for his investigation was the indecisive behavior of General Grant. Why, Eisenschiml repeatedly asked himself, did Grant first accept, then later reject the president's invitation to Ford's? Grant was no clumsy dogface, out of place away from a campfire. He was a West Point graduate who later became president. What made him commit such a grave breach of etiquette?

It struck Eisenschiml that only one man besides the president himself had the authority to prevent Grant from accepting the invitation. And only one

"Damn the Rebels, this is their work!"

Gideon Welles, Lincoln's Navy secretary

"Those men [the Confederates] . . . are public enemies. . . . But I know these men, sir. They are gentlemen, and incapable of being assassins."

Representative Thaddeus Stevens

Was Gen. Ulysses S. Grant, pictured here, ordered by Secretary of War Stanton not to attend the play with Lincoln?

man had the power and daring to shape later events to his liking.

That man was Secretary of War Edwin M. Stanton.

Here are the main threads of Eisenschiml's theory:

Stanton was driven by a lust for power. First as attorney general and then as war secretary, he used his position to turn himself into the most powerful member of Lincoln's administration. He even prolonged the war to increase the size and power of the military and to inflame the North against the South. Lincoln—whom Stanton despised anyhow—was beginning to see Stanton as a political adversary, opposed to his policy for peaceful reunion with the South. Stanton knew this and feared that Lincoln would remove him from office. At the height of his political clout, Stanton resolved that that would not happen. He was determined to protect his position.

Was There a Cover-Up?

If we assume that Stanton was behind the assassination, many of the blurry details become clear. Knowing Booth's plot, perhaps even planning it, Stanton made sure that the president had no protection at Ford's. He ordered Grant not to attend, denied the president the services of Major Eckert, and planted John Parker on the White House detail, later protecting him from the consequences of his neglect of duty. As the wounded president was dying, Stanton used his dictatorial powers to cover up his participation in the conspiracy. He withheld information from the newspapers, and, by failing to close off the Navy Yard Bridge, made sure that Booth would escape to the South, perhaps eventually to Europe.

In the meantime, he issued orders to General Augur and others designed to stall their pursuit of the assassin. Stanton was dismayed to find that Booth had broken his leg while escaping. His injury made his ultimate escape less likely and involved the unfortunate Dr. Mudd. Stanton, then, had to alter his plan. He not only had to find a way to silence Mudd, he also had to silence Booth, whose capture was becoming more probable with each day. Boston Corbett's confession that he shot Booth was a godsend, for it conveniently shifted suspicion away from Everton Conger, who did shoot Booth on orders from Stanton. Conger delivered up Booth's diary for Stanton to hide or destroy. The eight other conspirators could not be silenced in this way. They could, though, be gagged, held in solitary confinement, barred from stating their cases in open court, and sentenced either to an island prison off the coast of Florida or death by hanging. By promoting the view that the South was guilty, he kept suspicion from falling on himself.

This, in brief, is Eisenschiml's theory. He makes it clear that no *direct* evidence supports these claims. He stops short of stating this theory as a definite conclusion. But the circumstantial evidence Eisenschiml gathers against Stanton is convincing. The generally dim view that many historians take of the war secretary makes the Eisenschiml theory easier to accept.

More Theories

Not everyone, of course, accepts Eisenschiml's theory. Its leading opponent is historian William Hanchett. In his book, *The Lincoln Murder Conspiracies*, Hanchett questions each part of Eisenschiml's theory. Hanchett believes that Eisenschiml and his followers were trying to sensationalize the Lincoln assassination and that the theory rests on flimsy evidence and false logic. To each of the questions Eisenschiml raises, Hanchett provides an answer that does not rely on an elaborate conspiracy inside the government.

• Would Eckert, for example, have been able to foil the assassin? Probably not. Like Major Rathbone, he would have been the president's guest and so would have been sitting inside the box, not mounting guard outside it.

• Would another guard, sticking to his post, have prevented Booth from approaching the president? Maybe. But Booth was no lurking cutthroat. He was himself a popular, well-known public figure. The president's interest in actors and the theater increases the odds that Booth would have gained admittance to Lincoln's box no matter who was at the door.

• Did authorities ignore Weichmann's warning? Hanchett argues that Weichmann's accounts of his actions are unreliable.

• Did Stanton deliberately withhold Booth's identity from the newspapers? Perhaps, but only because he wanted to prevent lynch mobs from forming against a man who at the time was only a suspect.

• Did Stanton allow Booth to escape? No Union troops were in the area of the road south into Maryland and Virginia, so who was there for him to notify?

• Did Stanton order Conger, Corbett, or someone else to shoot Booth? No evidence supports this. The testimony of those present at Garrett's barn is contradictory.

• Did Stanton silence the other prisoners? He may have treated them harshly, but they had plenty of opportunities to tell their stories: when they were interrogated by the police, when they conferred with their lawyers in court, when they were visited by family or clergy in jail.

Thus Hanchett concludes: "When scrutinized point by point, Eisenschiml's grand conspiracy thus falls apart."

Stanton: The Leading Suspect?

In spite of Hanchett's harsh criticism of Eisenschiml, the theory that Stanton had a hand in the assassination has found its way into many books on the subject. Philip Van Doren Stern's biography, *The Man Who Killed Lincoln*, takes it as fact, for example, that War Department officials knew of Booth's plan to kill the president and that they aided his escape. In *The Mad Booths of Maryland*, Stanley Kimmel wonders why officials failed to round up the conspirators on the strength of Weichmann's information. Theodore Roscoe's *The Web of Conspiracy* amasses page after page of evidence supporting the main parts of Eisenschiml's theory.

To those who do not accept the view that Booth was acting alone, Stanton has been the leading suspect. But he was not the only administration official who has been fingered.

The Shelton Theory

Historian Vaughan Shelton offers another possibility. Like Eisenschiml, he began his investigation at a distinct starting point. For him, the key to the mystery lies in an unexpected quarter: Louis Paine, the only one of the accused no one felt any sympathy for. Paine was, after all, the only one of the eight with blood on his hands, the only one who could be directly linked to an act of violence on the night of April 14. So no one felt any pangs of remorse as he walked to the gallows on the afternoon of July 7.

Shelton, though, is certain that the Louis Paine who was tried and hanged was utterly innocent of any involvement in the plot to murder Lincoln.

Here is an overview of the conspiracy as Shelton sees it.

At the conspiracy's center was Col. Lafayette C. Baker, the "ruthless" head of the Secret Service. Like Stanton, Baker had taken advantage of the Civil War to increase his own power and authority. Commander of a shadow army of over two thousand, Baker was a figure to be reckoned with. With the war drawing to a close and Lincoln promising a peaceful reconciliation with the South, Baker knew

Some historians believe Louis Paine was innocent of any involvement in the conspiracy to kill Lincoln. Nonetheless, Paine was executed as a conspirator.

that he, like many other government officials, would soon see his ambitions ended.

Steeped as he was in the underworld of spies and counterspies, Baker knew John Surratt, a double agent who kept Baker informed of the progress of Booth's kidnap plot. When he could see that the plot was miscarrying, he brought in a Confederate deserter and spy named Lewis Powell. Powell's role was to take Booth in hand and somehow turn the actor's talk into action. With Baker's backing, Surratt began to plant in Booth's mind the belief that killing the president would make him famous. In Washington, Powell recruited Mary Surratt to the same end—to "mold" Booth's state of mind "to the

Hundreds of soldiers and citizens gather in Washington, D.C. for Lincoln's funeral, to pay tribute.

theme that Lincoln was the cause of all the nation's woes." He also recruited David Herold, whose main task would be to get rid of the assassin by poisoning his liquor while the two were in flight. With Booth dead, the case would be closed and no questions would be asked. In the meantime, Baker sought and received Stanton's silent cooperation in the plot—although Stanton did take the step of making sure that Lincoln had no protection when he went to Ford's.

A Side Arrangement

As Shelton describes it, "the plot was sound, relatively simple, and—under Powell's deft and subtle supervision—organized down to the last detail, Booth being led to believe that *he* was the leader and star of the company." But the plan did not go off without hitches. Shelton offers evidence that someone, probably Major Eckert, made a side arrangement with Powell to kill Secretary of State Seward. The attack would be timed to make it look like the same person, Booth, committed both crimes. But the attack on Seward took place at almost the same moment as that on Lincoln. This revealed that a conspiracy was at work.

The other hitch was that Booth survived. At Lloyd's tavern in Surrattsville, Herold laced a bottle of liquor with arsenic. But it was a bottle of whiskey, and Booth was a brandy drinker. Booth did not like whiskey, so he drank only enough to make him sick over the next several days, while Herold stood helplessly by.

Powell fled to Canada and never came under suspicion. The authorities stumbled across Louis Paine, who looked so much like Powell that they framed him for the crime. Meanwhile, Stanton, Baker, and Eckert were afraid that Booth would be found and the conspiracy would unravel. Baker, though, took steps to make sure that Booth did not fall into anyone's hands but his own. He interfered with the efforts of other military units until Everton

"This is a main thread in our study—the overwhelming evidence that Louis Paine didn't even know Booth, had nothing to do with the 'conspiracy' for which he and the other defendants were tried, and had not attacked Secretary of State Seward."
Historian Vaughan Shelton

"Shelton's explanation of the assassination . . . is worth consideration because it demonstrates the absurdities to which . . . obsession with conspiracy can drive . . . gullible minds."
Historian William Hanchett

Some historians say Confederate spy John H. Surratt received a letter from Secret Service director Col. Lafayette C. Baker less than a month before Lincoln's assassination. Why was the letter omitted from the military trial's official record?

Conger was able to track Booth down. Whether Boston Corbett fired the shot that killed Booth is unimportant. Booth was never to have been brought back to Washington alive.

According to Shelton, Baker's treachery did not end here. To satisfy the public's demand for prompt vengeance and to bring the affair to a dramatic conclusion, he engineered the conspiracy trial. The accused were hand-picked, and with Stanton's help, they were kept silent.

William Hanchett has less patience for Shelton's conspiracy theory than he does for Eisenschiml's. But rather than attacking the theory point by point, he examines closely the major piece of evidence on which it is built: a brief letter written to John Surratt from "R.D. Watson" summoning him to New York City. This letter was introduced as evidence in the conspiracy trial, but later omitted from the trial's official record, raising Shelton's suspicions.

The letter is dated March 19, 1865, right after the collapse of the kidnap scheme and just before the final act of the drama unfolded in Washington. Shelton submitted the letter to a handwriting analyst who concluded that its signature was Lafayette Baker's. The "important business" the letter referred to, in Shelton's view, had to be Baker's plan for murdering the president. He was writing under an assumed name to summon his agent to his headquarters to put the plan in motion.

A Grand Conspiracy?

Hanchett refutes Shelton's evidence in two ways. He hints, first, that Baker, in his role as chief of the Secret Service, could easily have had a legitimate reason for writing to Surratt, a known Confederate spy, under an assumed name. Second, he points out that the editors of the *Civil War Times Illustrated* tried to verify the handwriting analysis and were unable to do so. Their expert said that his analysis was "inconclusive." Thus, Hanchett concludes that Shelton erects a complex conspiracy theory on evidence at best flimsy and maybe even false. Further, he cites Shelton's theory as an example of how investigators seem almost to want to find a "grand conspiracy." In Hanchett's view, no grand conspiracy ever existed.

The theories of Eisenschiml and Shelton are major examples of the kinds of answers given to the question, "Who really was responsible for Lincoln's death?" And until historians can provide a complete record of the facts of Lincoln's murder, opinion will be divided between the belief that Booth hatched the conspiracy on his own and that he had the backing of powerful interests opposed to Lincoln. Investigators looking at the same record arrive at different conclusions because they have to approach the assassination more like detectives than historians. The historian strives to build theories based on a solid bedrock of evidence. The detective starts out with vaporous clues: the unexplained gap in the record, the odd contradiction in witnesses' accounts, the action that seems out of character. The historian takes what is known and tries to explain it; the detective is forever on a search for the unknown. The historian trades in facts, the detective in mysteries, in "What ifs . . . ?" The result in this case is a set of "maps" to the Lincoln assassination, each with different roads, each pointing to different destinations.

Six

Will We Ever Know for Sure?

(opposite page) Although Abraham Lincoln had a simple upbringing, he became one of the nation's most honored and respected presidents.

Like America's first president, George Washington, Abraham Lincoln has become a hero in a legend. His life is an example of the heights to which a simple man from an ordinary background can rise in America. His death, coming at the end of a long Civil War, turned him into a martyr for the Union and for the cause of ending slavery. The mystery that enfolds the circumstances of that death makes it almost impossible for the modern historian probing the record to separate fact from fiction.

For one thing, the record itself is inconsistent and contradictory. Historian Bruce Catton reminds us that examination of the diaries, books, articles, and court testimony of the people whose lives were touched by the assassination shows that at least twenty-five people say they helped carry the stricken president to the Petersen house across from Ford's. One says that the president was carried on a shutter torn from a window. Another says that he was carried in the rocking chair he was sitting in when he was shot. And at least eight people claim that they alone cradled the president's head as he was carried up to the room where he died. Eighty-four people say they were in the tiny room at one time or another that night. Three claim to have

Was it Booth's "simple conspiracy" that killed the president?

placed coins on the president's eyes the moment after he died. Conflicting testimony fails to confirm that Stanton was the one who said, "Now he belongs to the ages."

Witnesses to the crime itself are no more reliable. Fifteen hundred people were present in the theater, and yet even the "facts" of Booth's escape are in dispute. Not everyone agrees, for example, that he exclaimed "Sic semper tyrannis." Some state that he ran swiftly offstage, others that he crawled on his hands and knees. One witness stated that Booth slid down a flagpole to the stage, then crept away. One said that Booth was moaning, another that he said nothing at all.

And thus the reams of conflicting accounts of the events of those hours and days begin to pile up. The result for the modern historian is a maze, a hall of mirrors where recollection distorts what happened into bizarre and frightening shapes.

Questions Persist

Time, too, has proven to be the enemy of the historian of the Lincoln assassination. For time has enveloped the events of those days in mists that blur their outlines. For a record of the conversations that took place in the telegraph room of the War Department on the afternoon of April 14, historians rely on the forty-year-old remembrances of an aging civil servant. To get Edward Doherty's full account of the events at Garrett's barn, historians had to wait until 1890. Weichmann's account of his part in the story, though written in the 1890s, was not published until 1975. With each passing year, each passing decade, the haze surrounding the slain president and the people around him has grown thicker. But the questions persist:

Did Abraham Lincoln die as a result of a "simple conspiracy" hatched by one man with the aid of a small band of accomplices? Or was he betrayed by men within his own administration, the victim of a "grand conspiracy" that reached . . . who knows how far? Most Americans believed that John Wilkes Booth was acting on his own when he entered Ford's Theatre on the evening of April 14, 1865, and shot the president. But the many political assassinations of the 1960s, particularly that of President John F. Kennedy, revived in the popular mind the specter of conspiracy. Once again, a popular president—but one with enemies—was gunned down in public, apparently by a single crazed gunman. Once again, the assassin himself was shot to death under highly suspicious circumstances. Once again, investigation of the tragedy showed hundreds of gaps, inconsistencies, and unanswered questions. Once again, many people were convinced that a president died because powerful men feared that their power was in danger . . . that the gunman could not have acted alone . . . that a massive cover-up protected the guilty. The mind insists that such an act of violence has to have a complicated, far-reaching explanation. How can one person, armed with a weapon bought in a store, bring down the president of the United States?

And so, more than a century has passed, and no clear answer has formed to the question of who was really responsible for Lincoln's death. Like a restless ghost, the question still haunts Ford's Theatre and Baptist Alley, Tenth Street and H Street, the Maryland swamps, and the solemn tomb in Springfield, Illinois, where lies in rest the body of one of America's true legends, a man for the ages.

Lincoln's tomb in Springfield, Illinois. After more than a hundred years, few questions have been answered about his death.

For Further Exploration

Jim Bishop, *The Day Lincoln Was Shot*. New York: Harper and Brothers, 1955.

Champ Clark, *The Assassination: Death of the President*. Alexandria, VA: Time-Life Books, 1987.

Otto Eisenschiml, *Why Was Lincoln Murdered?* New York: Grosset and Dunlap, 1937.

Dorothy Kunhardt and Philip Kunhardt Jr., *Twenty Days*. New York: Harper and Row, 1965.

Theodore Roscoe, *The Web of Conspiracy*. Englewood Cliffs, NJ: Prentice Hall, 1959.

Carl Sandburg, *Abraham Lincoln, the War Years*, vol. IV. New York: Harcourt, Brace, 1939.

Works Consulted

David H. Bates, *Lincoln in the Telegraph Office*. New York: Appleton-Century, 1907.

George S. Bryan, *The Great American Myth*. New York: Carrick and Evans, 1940.

David M. DeWitt, *The Assassination of Lincoln and Its Expiation*. New York: Macmillan, 1909.

William Hanchett, *The Lincoln Murder Conspiracies*. Chicago: University of Chicago Press, 1983.

Stanley Kimmel, *The Mad Booths of Maryland*. New York: Bobbs-Mcrrill, 1940.

O.H. Oldroyd, *The Assassination of Abraham Lincoln*. Privately published, 1901.

Vaughan Shelton, *Mask for Treason*. Harrisburg, PA: Stackpole Books, 1965.

Philip Van Doren Stern, *The Man Who Killed Lincoln*. New York: Literary Guild, 1939.

William A. Tidwell, *Come Retribution: The Confederate Secret Service in the Assassination of Lincoln*. Jackson: University Press of Mississippi, 1988.

Thomas R. Turner, *Beware the People Weeping*. Baton Rouge: Louisiana State University Press, 1982.

Louis J. Weichmann, *A True History of the Assassination of Abraham Lincoln and of the Conspiracy of 1865*. New York: Knopf, 1975.

Index

About the Author

Michael O'Neal was born in Elyria, Ohio, in 1949. While he was an undergraduate English major at Bowling Green University, he developed a strong interest in books and writing. He served in the armed forces and then returned to Bowling Green to earn his doctorate. Currently, Michael is a teacher of English at Kirkwood Community College in Cedar Rapids, Iowa. He is the father of two children and lives in Iowa City with his wife.

Picture Credits